DATE DUE			

COMPANION TO RUSSIAN STUDIES
VOLUME 3

AN INTRODUCTION TO
RUSSIAN ART AND ARCHITECTURE
edited by Robert Auty and Dimitri Obolensky

COMPANION TO RUSSIAN STUDIES

AN INTRODUCTION TO

RUSSIAN ART AND ARCHITECTURE

EDITED BY
ROBERT AUTY
LATE PROFESSOR OF COMPARATIVE SLAVONIC PHILOLOGY
IN THE UNIVERSITY OF OXFORD
AND
DIMITRI OBOLENSKY
PROFESSOR OF RUSSIAN AND BALKAN HISTORY
IN THE UNIVERSITY OF OXFORD

WITH THE EDITORIAL ASSISTANCE OF
ANTHONY KINGSFORD

WITH CHAPTERS BY
ROBIN MILNER-GULLAND & JOHN BOWLT

CAMBRIDGE UNIVERSITY PRESS
CAMBRIDGE
LONDON · NEW YORK · NEW ROCHELLE
MELBOURNE · SYDNEY

Published by the Press Syndicate of the University of Cambridge
The Pitt Building, Trumpington Street, Cambridge CB2 1RP
32 East 57th Street, New York, NY 10022, USA
296 Beaconsfield Parade, Middle Park, Melbourne 3206, Australia

First published 1980

Set, printed and bound in Great Britain by
Fakenham Press Limited, Fakenham, Norfolk

Library of Congress Cataloguing in Publication Data
Main entry under title:
An introduction to Russian art and architecture.
(Companion to Russian studies; v. 3)
Includes bibliographies and index.
1. Art, Russian.   2. Architecture – Russia.
I. Auty, Robert.   II. Obolensky, Dimitri, 1918–.
III. Kingsford, Anthony.   IV. Series.
N6981.I57   709′.47   75–10691
ISBN 0 521 20895 5

CONTENTS

ILLUSTRATIONS

Note. The architectural plans and elevations, save where otherwise noted, are based on those in S. V. Bezsonov *et al., Istoriya russkoy arkhitektury* (Moscow, 1951, 1956). The dating of architectural monuments has caused continual difficulties, often with un-explained divergences between recognized authorities. The date of a building's inception, however, is generally more firmly established than that of its completion, and in most cases it is only the former (usually more significant from the point of view of the history of style, in any case) that has been indicated here. Page number precedes description in the following list.

vii

ILLUSTRATIONS

ILLUSTRATIONS

ILLUSTRATIONS

PREFACE

The *Companion to Russian Studies* aims at providing a first orientation for those embarking on the study of Russian civilization, past or present, in its most important aspects. It lays no claim to cover them all. While we hope that it will be of use to university students of Russian language and literature, Russian history, or Soviet affairs, it is equally directed to the general reader interested in these subjects. Each chapter seeks to offer a self-contained introduction to a particular topic; but the editors have not wished to impose a uniform pattern, and each author has been free to approach and present his subject in his own way. Particular care has been taken to provide up-to-date bibliographies, which are intended as a guide to further study. As is the way with collective works of this kind, the *Companion* has been some years in the making. We should like to express our gratitude to the contributors for their forbearance – sometimes sorely tried – in the face of difficulties and delays which have held up the completion of the enterprise. Economic considerations beyond our control have made it necessary to divide the contents of what had originally been planned as a single book into three volumes. The first is mainly concerned with the history of Russia and the Soviet Union; the second with Russian language and literature; the third with art and architecture. However, the three volumes, for which we share the editorial responsibility, should be regarded as complementary parts of a single whole.

We are grateful to all those at the Cambridge University Press who, over the years, have been involved in this project. Above all we wish to record our debt to Mr Anthony Kingsford, whose great experience in book production, unflagging energy, and expert knowledge of many aspects of Russian studies have been of the greatest value at every stage.

R.A.
D.O.

We wish to record our sorrow and sense of loss at the untimely death of Robert Auty on 18 August 1978, when this volume was still in proof.

D.O.
A.L.K.

TRANSLITERATION TABLE

		1	2
А	а	a	a
Б	б	b	b
В	в	v	v
Г	г	g	g
Д	д	d	d
Е	е	ye/e	je/e
Ё	ё	yo/o	jo/o
Ж	ж	zh	ž
З	з	z	z
И	и	i	i
Й	й	y	j
К	к	k	k
Л	л	l	l
М	м	m	m
Н	н	n	n
О	о	o	o
П	п	p	p
Р	р	r	r
С	с	s	s
Т	т	t	t
У	у	u	u
Ф	ф	f	f
Х	х	kh	ch
Ц	ц	ts	c
Ч	ч	ch	č
Ш	ш	sh	š
Щ	щ	shch	šč
	ъ	—	—
	ы	y	y
	ь	′	′
Э	э	e	e

TRANSLITERATION TABLE

Ю ю	yu	ju
Я я	ya	ja
(I i)	i	i
(Ѣ ѣ)	ě	ě
(Ѳ ѳ)	f	f
(V v)	i	i

The transliteration system given in column 1 is used in all sections of the *Companion* except Volume 2, chapter 1, *The Russian Language*, where the 'philological' system given in column 2 is employed. The bracketed letters at the end of the alphabet were discontinued by the spelling reform of 1917–18.

ye (*je*) is written for Cyrillic e initially, after vowels, and after ъ and ь. *o* appears for ё after ж, ч, ш, щ. In proper names final -ый, -ий is simplified to -*y*.

Proper names or titles which have a generally accepted anglicized form are usually given in that form, e.g. Benoit, Chagall, Deineke, Diaghilev, Dimitri, Hermitage, Likhachev, Lissitzky, Meyerhold, Moscow, Peterhof, Sophia.

1

ART AND ARCHITECTURE OF OLD RUSSIA, 988-1700

Introduction

For almost a millennium, art and architecture have flourished in Russia
with a consistency of high achievement unmatched by Russian literature,
music or thought, whose notable successes have been won only against
a background of erratic and, on the whole, rather tardy development.
There is some sense in considering the visual arts the central area, even
the pace-setter, of Russian culture through most of its long history: the
wordless language of paintings and buildings compensates for the
notorious 'intellectual silence' of Old Russia, so often noted by foreigners,
and it is able to tell us what is distinctively Russian about such moments
of apparently thorough integration with the western cultural system as the
mid-eighteenth and early twentieth centuries. In particular Russian
architecture – cheerful, modest and down-to-earth, seldom reaching
towards grandeur or sublimity – has a quite remarkable record of vigour
and inventiveness over the centuries; while Russian painting has had at
least two moments (in the early fifteenth century and during the 1910s)
when it could be reasonably argued to have led the whole of Europe.

This long and splendid artistic tradition, for quite understandable
historical and geographical reasons, is still inadequately known abroad.
This survey is certainly no substitute for the rigorous, detailed, and up-to-
date study of Old Russian art which we need in English; what it does aim
to do is to tell in concise fashion what happened when, to trace the development of styles and genres, to give an indication of what seems art-historic-
ally important and why, and lastly to contradict a few prevalent myths and
locate the chief unresolved problems. In the process much has had to be
ignored or summarily treated: in particular folk art, the minor and
applied arts, and the tradition of architecture in wood get far less attention
than they would ideally have deserved. I have tried to bear in mind the
reader with a fair general knowledge of art (particularly the potential
visitor to Russia) who will not be familiar with the development of Russian
art or its chief characteristics at various times; for this reason I have
discussed the different branches of art according to a periodization which,

1

even if unusual in some respects, I believe to be the most helpful for the purpose. Some attempt – necessarily brief – has been made to see Russian art as part of a general pattern of culture, in both a national and a European setting.

Note that where a single date has been given to a building, this refers to the beginning of its construction unless otherwise indicated.

Old Russian art: its characteristics, scope and international setting

The art of Russia before the eighteenth century was broadly (with due qualifications) a 'medieval' art. It was functional, having a necessary role to fulfil within a self-sufficient cultural system. It held firmly to tradition, and was exercised through a well-developed set of genres, conventions and symbols. It attended to the universal and eternal rather than to the transient and the accidental. Its practitioners were more concerned to execute a necessary task in the proper manner than to express an individual personality. It was saturated with its society's religion. It lacked several of the art-forms that we take for granted in secularized, post-Renaissance Europe; it neither knew nor would have had a use for the systematic perspective and illusionistic techniques of post-Renaissance painting. Until almost the end of the seventeenth century, architecture seems to have retained medieval 'rule of thumb' methods of construction.

However, this art should not be thought of as unsophisticated or primitively spontaneous. There was a clear distinction between 'high' and folk art, even if from time to time the two spheres affected or inter-penetrated each other. Nor was it undifferentiated: there were 'metro-politan' and 'provincial' manners, allowing a variety of intermediate possibilities. It was not mechanical: no two medieval pictures or buildings are identical; it was not depersonalized, as there was scope, if limited, for the exercise of artistic individuality – the names of leading artists (particularly after the fourteenth century) are often known to us, and in many cases we can form an impression of their style. It was not exclusively in the hands of monks or clerics: several important artists were probably laymen (Theophanes, Dionisy). Its aims and methods were not 'anti-realistic', at least not in the eyes of its practitioners. It was not 'unpro-gressive', despite the stubborn myth that Byzantine/Orthodox art and architecture are no more than variations on a theme: it shows well-marked evolutionary stages, though the transitions between them are gradual rather than violent. Lastly, it would be wrong to think of it as utterly cut off from our own aesthetic categories and traditions: its principles, ideals and methods are descended, if at one or more remove,

2

from classical antiquity. Old Russian writers frequently and touchingly speak of beauty in relation to the works of art of their age, and what they admire turns out on the whole to correspond with what we admire.

The adoption of Christianity on the Byzantine model as the Russian state religion in or about 988 meant the 'importing' of an entire cultural system, including a varied and highly-developed art. There is no reason to suppose the soil of Russia was unprepared for this. Though our evidence for the condition of art in pagan Russia is scanty, we can reasonably suppose it flourished, at least on a 'folk' level. Its most impressive material remains are carved idols (popularly known as *kamennyye baby*, stone women). There was certainly a well-developed architecture in wood, and masonry buildings are now known to have existed. In any case, Christianity had been gradually establishing a foothold in Kiev many decades before the official conversion.

Russia joined the Byzantine 'cultural commonwealth' at a favourable moment. A Slavonic sub-community, using its own language for liturgy and literature, already existed within it. Byzantium, at the height of its early medieval vigour, had evolved the 'classic' forms of its art during the previous century or so. Those splendidly flexible and simple architectural forms, the 'cross-domed' and 'cross-in-square' church, had been stabilized as the typical patterns of high-Byzantine ecclesiastical architecture; they, and not the older, alternative form of the basilica, were to establish a domination in Russia unchallenged for over 500 years. The interior walls of such churches were decorated, according to an impressive scheme (of symbolic significance), with glass mosaic or – as soon became normal in Russia – with true fresco. The technique of fresco-painting encouraged a bold and expressive handling of the medium. Small teams of artists, on occasion travelling far afield, would complete the decoration of a church in a single summer if possible, sometimes several years after it had been built. Meanwhile it would be decorated with *icons* (i.e. 'images') – the third great form of Orthodox pictorial art. These often quite large panels (the ancestors of modern 'easel paintings', curious as it may seem) normally consist of one or more wooden boards, with painting in tempera on a fine plaster ground; they carried representations of sacred personages and events, and though not in themselves worshipped, they were venerated as the channel through which worshipper could reach saint and vice versa. The general forms of any given representation were not subject to alteration at whim (going back as several of them supposedly did to St Luke, eyewitness of the scenes he painted). Byzantine icons of high artistic quality – particularly from before the fourteenth century – are very few, and the fortunate preservation of several fine examples would alone have

3

ensured Russia a unique importance for our understanding of medieval Orthodox art. Icons shared with book illuminations (another well-developed Byzantine art, particularly significant for its role in preserving classical-antique models of painting) an easy portability and high prestige; through them the example of 'metropolitan' painting, or for that matter innovations of style and iconography, could be transmitted to all parts of the Orthodox world, counterbalancing centrifugal and provincializing tendencies. The marvellously skilful Byzantine so-called 'minor arts' – low-relief carvings in ivory, silver and gold objects, jewellery, enamels – played something of the same role.

The Byzantine connexion conditioned the nature of Old Russian art, up to and even after the trauma of 1453, when Constantinople fell. It would be wrong to treat Old Russian art as synonymous with Byzantine – each nation of the Orthodox community had its own artistic development, within certain overall limits – but it would be equally wrong to regard it as the branch of a tree, developing out of and away from Byzantium. Old Russia was able, until the fifteenth century, to refresh itself through renewals of contact, not only with Constantinople, but with other Orthodox lands (notably with the South Slavs of Serbia and Bulgaria). Other international contacts – particularly with western Europe in its Romanesque, Gothic and Renaissance phases – had effects which, if not purely fortuitous, were nevertheless essentially limited in their cultural significance, few in number and easily definable. With the remoter Christian lands of Transcaucasia, as with the Scandinavian north, few if any artistic contacts can be demonstrated (though some commentators have tried). And oddly enough (in view of geographical propinquity and of the 240 years of subjection to the Tatars), Russia was perhaps less open to cultural influence from the Moslem lands than any country in Europe. The favourite nineteenth-century assumption that Russian art, and culture as a whole, was essentially 'oriental' turns out to be without any historical basis.

Medieval Russia has left a relatively rich artistic heritage: one that, until in the later fifteenth and sixteenth centuries the achievements of the Florentine Renaissance spread through the west, in no way lagged behind the rest of Europe – and even in its lengthy decline showed moments of inspiration. Yet it is worth reminding ourselves from time to time of some of its achievements which are irreparably lost to us. From before 1600 we have scarcely any surviving secular architecture: of the splendid palaces of the Kievan and Vladimir Grand Princes, with their fine furnishings and extensive frescoes, we know tantalizingly little, even from literary sources. The wooden architecture of the same period, whether popular or sophisticated, has almost all perished: we know only that it must have been highly inventive and adaptable. Old Russian sculpture has survived fragmentarily and probably not representatively. From four decades at the beginnings of Russian post-conversion art (996–1036) our knowledge is quite blank.

In modern times, too, war, carelessness and wanton destruction have lost for us some of the greatest buildings and paintings that had been spared by previous ages; but that is another story.

The discovery of Old Russian art

Before the present century the achievements of Old Russian art and architecture were scarcely appreciated or even properly accessible. Underrated by the Russians themselves (who were conscious of the excessive and stifling duration of their 'medieval' past), known to few foreigners in a position to evaluate them, the numerous buildings and paintings that antedated the westernizing reforms of the seventeenth and eighteenth centuries were in any case generally deformed by later alterations, accretions and restorations. The materials for a just assessment, or for that matter a history, of Old Russian art were simply not available.

Even had they been so, it may be doubted whether nineteenth-century taste would have reacted understandingly, let alone enthusiastically, to them. Napoleon, having entered Moscow, is reported to have ordered 'that mosque' (meaning the Church of Basil the Blessed in Red Square) to be removed. He was no doubt not alone in thinking Old Russian building uncouth and oriental – though it is neither. Nevertheless, a current of antiquarian interest stemming from the time (and personal initiative) of Catherine the Great ensured the preservation of some buildings and the detailed recording of others, as well as more doubtful projects such as Nicholas I's radical restoration of the St Demetrius Cathedral in Vladimir. When in the 1880s V. Vasnetsov and the 'Abramtsevo colony' built a small church in a pleasant pastiche of Old Russian style, it became evident that such architecture could have real aesthetic significance for sophisticated members of the generation out of which the 'modern movement' sprang. Yet as regards Old Russian painting, knowledge and appreciation were rudimentary even at the end of the nineteenth century. In particular the surviving icons and frescoes from the greatest age of Old Russian pictorial art (the fourteenth and fifteenth centuries) were still without exception obscured by grime or overpainting. Andrey Rublyov, whose work is the culmination of that age, had sunk to a figure of legend; it was the cleaning (in 1904) of his famous 'Old Testament Trinity' icon, from the Trinity Monastery of St Sergius, that marked the start of true scholarly investigation into his work and the nature of Old Russian painting in general. If one man's contribution to this process should be singled out, it must be that of Igor' Grabar' – himself an excellent painter – who for decades bore the heaviest burdens in the fields both of restoration and research. However, the rediscovery of Old Russian art required not simply the dedication of individuals, but a revolution in aesthetic taste. This came about with the rise of 'modernism' in the years preceding the First World War. The dominance of Renaissance 'picture-space' and naturalism over serious art was shattered, and qualities such as the static stylization and the free play of line and colour typical of Old Russian painting could at last be appreciated for their aesthetic worth. Too much, indeed, has often been made of some of these qualities: the 'primitivism' of icon-painting (gauged on the basis of late or provincial examples) can easily be overestimated, and the nature of Old Russian art thereby seriously misjudged.

From the 1910s Old Russian paintings were systematically collected (or, in the case of wall-paintings, identified) and cleaned – a process which is continuing to the present day, but as early as the 1920s had produced a remarkable body of material on which scholarly work could be done. The serious investigation of Old Russian architecture, on the other hand, lagged a little: to re-establish and restore the early aspect of a building is no small task. Paradoxically, the destruction suffered by many important Old Russian buildings during the Second World War had some positive effects: it permitted, for example, the investigation into the original form of the partially-destroyed Pyatnitsky Church in Chernigov, which has helped us radically to revise our ideas about the evolution of medieval architecture. Since the war, in fact, previous notions of what happened to architecture in the important age from the twelfth to the fifteenth centuries have been entirely superseded, and this has had interesting implications for the general history of Russian culture.

Much has been discovered or evaluated very recently; many problems are still debatable, and many tasks remain. The original ground-plan of so important a building as the St Sophia Cathedral in Novgorod, for example, was only established (despite widely differing speculations through the years) when central heating was installed there in the 1960s. The wealth of Old Russian sculpture is only slowly becoming known: older books denied its very existence, and treated the famous carvings of Vladimir–Suzdal' (still the subject of controversy) as utterly exceptional. Frescoes as important as those of the Mirozhsky Monastery at Pskov have yet to be properly cleared from overpainting. Soviet archaeology is continually turning up new, and sometimes surprising, facts. Though the history and evaluation of Old Russian art and architecture can now be undertaken, we should be rash to regard even their basic outlines as finally established and agreed. The present survey aims not so much to make quasi-definitive judgements on doubtful points as to present the development of early Russian art in the light of recent research and current critical appreciation.

Kievan Russia: late tenth to early twelfth centuries

From the first century or so of Christianized Russia – the 'classic' period of the Kievan state – there survive: less than a dozen important churches; one great combined fresco and mosaic decorative cycle, and several other fragments of mural painting and mosaic; some of the earliest illuminated books in the Church Slavonic language; a couple of small carved-stone icons; various archaeological remains, including the foundations of domestic and defensive structures. Thus we have enough material to allow us to characterize the art and architecture of the age, while considerable gaps in our knowledge have to be recognized. Literary sources help us in some cases to fill these; but as fundamental a problem as (for example) the extent of Bulgaria's role in the transmission to Russia of the Orthodox cultural system, including its art, remains tantalizingly insoluble.

After the proclamation of Orthodox Christianity as the Kievan state religion, Vladimir took immediate steps to construct in his capital a suitably impressive cathedral. Byzantine experts were brought in to direct the work, which was completed in 996. We cannot know precisely what this building, the so-called Desyatinnaya ('Tithe') Church, dedicated to the Dormition, looked like, for it collapsed at the time of the Tatar invasion. But its foundations have been excavated in modern times, and reveal a fairly large, three-nave church with surrounding galleries, probably of the normal Byzantine cross-in-square plan. Already the typical external pattern of early Kievan masonry is found here: narrow horizontal layers of brickwork separated by wide bands of pinkish mortar (which conceal from the outside every other row of bricks) giving a 'striped' appearance to wall surfaces. In the next century this technique becomes for a time characteristic of Byzantine architecture too, and 'reverse influence' from Kiev (however improbable prima facie) has been suggested. The Tithe Church was notable for its rich decoration, and interesting scraps of décor, including floor-mosaic and frescoes, have been found in its ruins.

There follows a gap in our knowledge of Kievan art nearly half-a-century long – until the intense building activity of the late 1030s under Yaroslav. It is customary to begin any account of the surviving monuments with the famous church of St Sophia (i.e. Holy Wisdom), begun in 1037. In fact, however, primacy belongs to the second city of Kievan Russia, Chernigov, whose great Transfiguration (Spaso-Preobrazhensky) Cathedral was completed in, or soon after, 1036. It also boasts the earliest surviving Russian mural painting: a faded but noble half-figure of St Thekla. The ground-plan of this fine building is unique in the Russian lands. Externally, it

7

Constantinople, Kilise Cami (eleventh or twelfth century): ground-plan of Byzantine cross-in-square church, with narthex and later exonarthex (after A. I. Nekrasov).

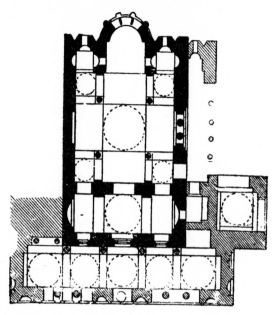

Pereyaslavl'-Zalesskiy, Transfiguration Cathedral (1152): ground-plan of Russian cross-in-square church, single dome, no narthex.

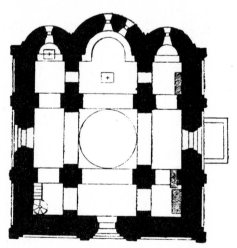

appears to be a normal five-domed cross-in-square church; inside, two curtain walls, separating the naves at either side of the crossing and pierced by arcades at floor and gallery level, give the impression of a domed basilica.

In the space of a few years during the eleventh century three major cathedrals, all dedicated to St Sophia, were built in the greatest cities of south, west and north Russia – at Kiev, Polotsk (1044) and Novgorod (1045). The dedication is an obvious reminiscence of Constantinople, and perhaps reflects Graecophile tendencies in eleventh-century Russia as well as a strongly-rooted sense of national pride (illustrated in contemporary literature by the Metropolitan Hilarion's *Sermon on Law and Grace*). The Kiev Sophia was, and remained, the greatest building of Old Russia in prestige, in richness of ornamentation, and (with its outer galleries that were soon incorporated into the main building) in size. The focus of secular as well as sacred life in medieval Kiev, it still today (as a museum) seems more numinous with the spirit of early Russia than any other spot. Perhaps this effect is actually aided rather than hindered by the seventeenth-century restorations and accretions which have obliterated its original outer form, thereby so surprisingly concealing the almost perfectly preserved interior.

St Sophia of Kiev is one of the handful of great middle-Byzantine buildings which represent the finest European artistic achievement of the early Middle Ages. But though it stands beside Daphni and Hosios Lukas in the history of Orthodox art, and like them displays within its walls a great mosaic cycle of pure high-Byzantine inspiration, it is a building which, from a Byzantine viewpoint, has certain very distinctive features;

Chernigov, Transfiguration Cathedral (*c.* 1036): ground-plan.

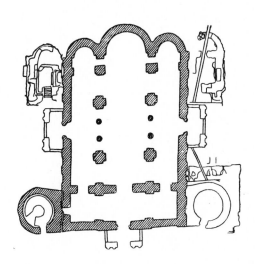

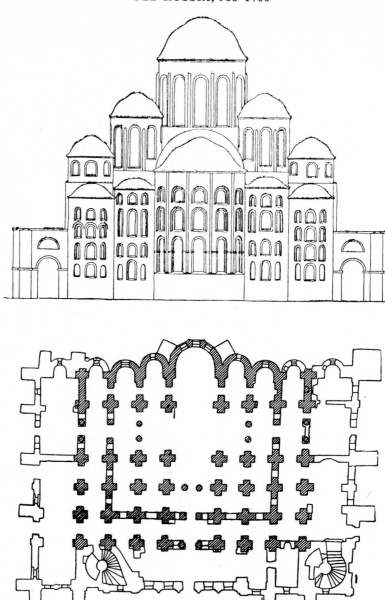

Kiev, St Sophia (1037): reconstruction of east façade and ground-plan (eleventh-century structure shaded).

while from a Russian viewpoint it exemplifies, for all its uniqueness, characteristics which were to give Russian architecture some of its distinctive flavour for the next half-millennium. Its thirteen domes (a number unequalled in any other surviving building of the Byzantine world) were so grouped – on unusually tall drums – as to lend St Sophia a strongly pyramidal outline when its present-day accretions are discounted. This pyramidality is most potently determined, however, through the 'stepped' roofline of the galleries and naves, whose successively-higher arches were visible externally. This effect, foreign to standard Byzantine practice of the age, comes, as we shall see, to have far-reaching significance in late-medieval Russian architecture. External effect – achieved not only through overall outline and picturesque disposal of the domes, but through the characteristic polychrome masonry described above, and the rows of blind niches covering the apsidal wall – is most important in St Sophia, and remains so in most Russian medieval architecture (this feature it shares with the churches of Serbia and Bulgaria, and with Byzantine architecture in its later phase). No strivings towards the longitudinal form of the basilica – observable even in typical cross-domed Byzantine churches – can be detected in the Kiev St Sophia. Its naves, indeed, are remarkably short for so wide a building; it does not create its impression of size and grandeur through the long vistas of a tall Romanesque or Gothic nave, but through careful, intimate proportion, and the strongly centralized plan that draws the visitor's gaze upwards rather than along. Centralization is emphasized by its wider transepts and central nave, intersected by double-arcaded curtain-walls like those in the Transfiguration Cathedral in Chernigov, but here standing a bay further back so as to preserve the plan of a short-armed cross about the central dome (the western curtain-wall, which bore part of a remarkable group portrait of Yaroslav's family, has unfortunately not been preserved). Like the outer galleries, two solid staircase-towers were soon added to the original fabric at the western corners: such towers are particularly characteristic of the early buildings of Kievan Russia.

The décor of St Sophia combined a cycle of mosaics (centred on the most important parts of the building – the dome and main apse) with fresco paintings; such a scheme within one church is rare in extant Byzantine monuments. As at the Tithe Church, Byzantine masters must have set up the mosaic workshop, though our written sources do not record this. The mosaics – rather stiff and archaic for their time, but impressive for all that – follow normal Byzantine disposition and iconography; the fresco cycle (not all of which has yet been cleaned) is treated more freely. For us today the most remarkable part of the entire décor may be the small, faded paintings within the staircase towers, whence galleries once led to the prince's palace-complex. These are unique not only in Russia but in

Kiev, St Sophia (1037): apse with mosaic of the Virgin and Communion of the Apostles; seventeenth-century icon-screen.

the Byzantine world as surviving examples of secular mural painting. They show scenes from the games at the Hippodrome in Constantinople, hunting scenes, musicians with their instruments (including a proto-violin and an organ), jesters: the unifying symbolic theme would appear to be the glorification of imperial authority. They are executed in an expressive, coarse linear style very different from the sophistication of the frescoes within the cathedral proper.

The cathedrals of St Sophia at Polotsk and Novgorod were also originally large five-naved structures. That of Polotsk has suffered drastic damage and alteration over the centuries. The Novgorod Sophia, however, has retained its external form better than that of Kiev; recent research indicates that it was designed with its present galleries and tower. Internally it has lost much, but not all, of its frescoed décor. With a ground-plan generally similar to that of its Kievan predecessor, it nevertheless creates a quite different architectural impression: its proportions are taller and narrower, the exterior starkly imposing, with little attempt to ingratiate either through ornament or through well-calculated articulation of the façades. Other early Novgorod churches that have survived (in the Yur'yev and Antonov Monasteries and the *Yaroslavovo dvorishche*) show a similar uncompromising cragginess; their stonework and pink, smoothed mortar were originally exposed, not as now stuccoed and whitewashed.

Kiev, mosaics from St Michael: head of an apostle (early twelfth century).

Kiev, staircase tower of St Sophia: fresco of a musician (eleventh or twelfth century).

We cannot be certain when the characteristic external 'onion dome' arose, but it probably evolved in Novgorod in pre-Tatar times. It is a moot point whether this feature, and the general narrow proportions of Novgorod architecture, owe anything to the example of the native wooden architecture of the Russian north; interestingly, we learn from the chronicles that the Novgorod Sophia of 1044 replaced a multi-topped wooden predecessor.

In Kiev the next major church to be built after St Sophia was the Cathedral of the Dormition (Uspensky Sobor) in the Pechersky (Cave) Monastery, the most important religious and intellectual centre of Kiev Rus'. Its simple, airy four-column cross-in-square plan became almost the standard type of medium-sized Old Russian churches. It is recorded that 'Greek' artists decorated it in 1083–9; alas, the cathedral was blown up during the recent war, without any real scholarly study of it having been made. Another lamentable loss from the architecture of the time was the cathedral of the St Michael 'Golden-topped' (Zlatoverkhiy) Monastery, founded in 1108, and identified by some writers with the earlier Monastery of St Demetrius. It was demolished by the Kiev city authorities in 1934; luckily art-historians managed to save its splendid mosaics, remnants of the only pictorial mosaic cycle other than that of St Sophia to have survived on Russian soil into modern times. Again Byzantines (perhaps from among those who had worked in the Pechersky Monastery) can be supposed to have had a hand in their making, and again mosaics were juxtaposed with frescoes. Though the well-known figure of St Demetrius

Novgorod, Cathedral of St George in Yur'yev Monastery (1119): reconstruction with original roofline.

Kiev, Dormition Cathedral in the Pechersky Monastery (1073): ground-plan.

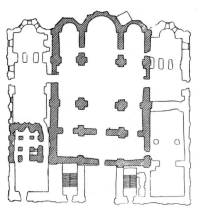

(now in Moscow) has the brooding monumentality of early Kiev, the main surviving mosaic scene – representing the Communion of the Apostles – differs interestingly from the same subject in the apse of St Sophia (in whose galleries the St Michael mosaics are now mostly housed). The figures are less schematically disposed; they are executed less rigidly, more sinuously, with stronger linear emphasis and a somewhat different – deeper and richer in colour, though tonally less varied – palette. Many people will find them on a higher artistic plane than those of St Sophia, and they are particularly remarkable in the degree to which they presage the developments in art associated with the middle and later twelfth century.

Pictorial mosaic was probably never employed again in medieval Russia. Its cost was colossal; without a continuous native tradition, patrons had to import Byzantine masters and to set up a glass factory if they wished to commission a mosaic cycle. But non-figurative mosaic – intricate patterns inset into slabs of stone or cement, and decorating not only floors but the lower part of walls – had a long, and still under-investigated, life in Kievan Russia. Many original ceramic-mosaic slabs of this kind survive in the Novgorod Sophia, and have recently been dated to the mid- or later twelfth century. However, even at this early stage it was evident that fresco-painting was to become the essential Russian decorative art. What it might lack in pomp it made up in subtlety, flexibility and availability. Already in the first century or so after Vladimir's conversion considerable stylistic variety is to be found, particularly in surviving frescoes from Novgorod; we encounter both the elegantly classical features associated with the 'metropolitan' style of Constantinople, and at the opposite extreme the heavily outlined, distorted, ungainly but expressive characteristics of the provincial Orthodox manner often (but not altogether appropriately) designated as the 'Oriental' or 'East Christian' style. Nevertheless we should exercise great caution in speaking of such-and-such stylistic influences on Old Russian painting of this period, other than that from Byzantium; too many links in our chains are missing.

Illustrated manuscripts from the early Kievan period are few in number but high in quality. The famous Ostromir Codex (1056–7) has fine Byzantine-style decorative initials and full-page miniatures, as does Svyatoslav's Compendium (*Izbornik*) of 1073. The remarkable, if faded, illustration of St John in the Priest Domka's Gospels probably dates from around 1100, and shows pronounced 'provincial-expressive' traits.

Unfortunately no surviving Russian religious panel-paintings can be dated with certainty to this period,[1] though a twelfth-century example

---

[1] Much of the paintwork of the icon of SS Peter and Paul in the Novgorod Museum may date back as far as the late eleventh century, however.

such as the great 'Ustyug Annunciation' surely carries on its traditions; we know that icon-painting flourished then, and it was of course a necessary part of the Orthodox cultural system. Some small items of metal, enamel and stone work display vigorous technical mastery. Decorative low-relief carving on stone (even, on occasion, imported marble) is to be found in the Kiev Sophia and some other major churches.

Kievan and Vladimir Russia: early twelfth to mid-thirteenth centuries

The term 'Kievan' is ordinarily applied to Russia before the Tatar invasions and conquest of *c.* 1240. Throughout that time Kiev remained a great city, but its hegemony over the Russian lands was weakened as early as the years following Yaroslav's death (1054), and despite the revival under Vladimir Monomakh in the early twelfth century it never regained its old prestige. After Monomakh its very status as capital was put in question, when the city of Vladimir was adopted as the seat of government by his grandson Andrey Bogolyubsky (1157–74). All this had a considerable effect on Russian art of the twelfth century. A loosening of central ties, politically fatal to the integrity of Rus' (as the Tatar conquest was to demonstrate), brought about on the credit side an unprecedented number of local artistic centres, each rivalling its neighbours in its contribution to the sudden variety of Russian artistic achievement at the time. And Vladimir with its subsidiary towns became a new artistic focus, outshining even Novgorod and Kiev; out of the culture of Vladimir that of Moscow was to grow.

Irrespective of local conditions in Russia a new artistic language was being formulated in the early to middle twelfth century throughout the Orthodox world, and indeed in Europe as a whole. This, the moment when northern Romanesque art entered its last and most exuberant phase, when early Gothic was establishing itself in the Île de France, when Italy and Provence saw the last classical 'renascence' before the Renaissance proper, was a period of comparable importance in the development of Byzantine art. The unemotional rigidity of the high-Byzantine representational system cracks; a new humanity enters the depiction of human faces, a new fluidity and dynamism suffuses bodies and drapery. The way has been opened towards the 'Palaeologan' art of the thirteenth to fifteenth centuries which in certain respects anticipated, and perhaps affected, that of early Renaissance Europe. Nevertheless the best features of tenth–eleventh-century art are not yet abandoned; classic principles are reanimated and reasserted. High Byzantine monumentality and serenity remain, invigorated by new flexibility and variegation.

Russia experienced this spirit as early as any of the Orthodox lands; it

16

was a broad cultural movement (as Roman Jakobson has pointed out), which brought a new intricacy, grace and sophistication to art and literature equally. There is considerable pathos (felt by men of the time) in the dichotomy between this cultural efflorescence and the disruptive forces at work in the Russian state – heightened from a modern viewpoint by knowledge of the disaster to come.

'Ustyug Annunciation' icon (twelfth century): detail.

In Kiev and neighbouring lands artistic activity continued, though on a smaller scale than hitherto. The late twelfth-century frescoes in the Kievan Church of St Cyril and elsewhere have, regrettably, not yet been properly restored or published; they promise interesting finds. But the twelfth-century architecture of southern Russia, long neglected, has emerged from research of the last twenty-five years as astonishingly forward-looking and innovatory. The chief discoveries have been made in Chernigov, which preserves an important series of pre-Tatar buildings. The St Paraskeva-Pyatnitsa Church, built *c.* 1200 but restored (like all old buildings of the area) during the Baroque period, was partially destroyed in the Second World War: it unexpectedly revealed in its damaged state a design that anticipates features of early Muscovite architecture by 200 years. Three stepped tiers of arches – noticeably pointed, though no Gothic influence is demonstrable – rise to a central dome in a strongly pyramidal and dynamic silhouette. The foundations of churches conjectured to have been of similar shape (though with interesting variants of plan) have since been excavated in the nearby cities of Novgorod-Seversk and Putivl'. There can be little doubt that this group of buildings, rather than, as once was thought, the Serbian church of Gračanica (1315), represents a direct ancestor of all those that were to be adorned with 'stepped' arches (*zakomary* and *kokoshniki*) in Muscovy right up to the seventeenth century. Stepped arches of a somewhat different kind, similarly used both constructively and ornamentally, have recently been discovered also in the original form of two twelfth-century churches in west Russia:

Chernigov, Church of St Paraskeva-Pyatnitsa (*c.* 1200): reconstruction of east façade.

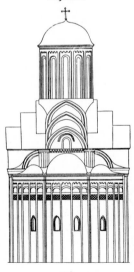

18

the Yefrosin'yev Monastery at Polotsk (mid-twelfth century), and the Cathedral of Michael the Archangel (also called the Svirskaya Church, 1191), at Smolensk. The latter's splendidly forceful centrality and pyramidality are enhanced by lower porches in all three side walls, having also the effect with the central apse of giving a more emphatically cross-shaped plan to its basic cross-in-square; this plan reappears in later churches such as Yur'yev-Pol'sky and Kovalyovo. The triple-centred curve of its façade anticipates a favourite design of later Novgorod buildings.

Novgorod itself seems to have remained architecturally rather conservative until the turn of the twelfth–thirteenth centuries. A 'standard type' of simple church evolved there: a four-column cross-in-square, with three apses, its façades articulated (in correspondence with the interior) into three round-headed bays, separated by pilaster strips, with the roofline following the heads of these bays (*zakomary*), and with little

(*Left*) Polotsk, Cathedral of Yefrosin'yev Monastery (1150s): reconstruction of west façade. (*Right*) Smolensk, Cathedral of Michael the Archangel, or Svirskaya Church (1191): reconstruction.

else by way of exterior decoration. The most famous example of this modest but self-assured type is the Church of the Saviour on the Nereditsa Hill (Spas na Nereditse) near Novgorod (1198). The St Paraskeva Church of 1207, however, had novel features reminiscent of the Smolensk 'Svirskaya'. In Pskov, Novgorod's 'younger brother', the cathedral of the Mirozhsky Monastery (*c.* 1156) shows a variant of some importance: the 'corner-compartments' within the basic square were walled off as separate small rooms and originally roofed at a lower level, emphasizing the cross-shaped element of the basic plan.

None of these buildings is large by the standards of the preceding age. After the cathedral of the Yur'yev Monastery (1119) no more multi-domed churches are known to us – with one important exception – from before the Tatar conquest. This smaller-scale building activity reflects changed political circumstances, shortage of funds, but also the growing habit of constructing lesser churches out of brick or stone instead of (as before) wood. The little Church of St Elijah (Il'inskaya) at Chernigov is important: it has no piers at all, the drum of its dome resting on small arches springing from the interior wall. Concentration on smaller, single-domed churches encouraged the experiments mentioned above in the direction of centralization, pyramidality, exterior elegance and well-proportioned intimacy.

Novgorod, Church of the Saviour, Nereditsa (1198): south façade.

The one, exceptional, five-domed church of the time is of course the great Dormition (Uspensky) Cathedral at Vladimir, as remodelled and extended in 1189 by Andrey Bogolyubsky's son Vsevolod. Adding a whole new bay to the north, south and west of Andrey's three-naved church (1158), Vsevolod with an inspired touch allowed the original three *zakomary* to remain visible above and behind his new facades, thus echoing the 'stepped' vaults of the Kiev Sophia. Half-a-dozen surviving churches from the Vladimir lands represent in fact the most remarkable expression of the late Kievan period's visual taste, placing it on a par with the highest achievements of contemporary medieval Europe.

Our knowledge of the Vladimir principality's architecture begins with two churches of 1152, at Pereyaslavl'-Zalessky and Kideksha. They are modest in scale, and in fact very similar (though less rough-hewn) to Novgorod churches of the late twelfth-century 'standard pattern' as discussed above. But gradually decorative elements grow and the simple type is transformed – while preserving the integrity of its harmonious proportions. Thus a mere string-course half-way up the façade at Pereyaslavl' is elaborated into a modest frieze at Kideksha, a full-scale arcade of engaged columns on the Vladimir Dormition, which in turn rest on carved masks at the Church on the Nerl' (Pokrov na Nerli, 1165), grows elaborate decorative carving and sculptured infilling on the Vladimir St Demetrius Cathedral (1194), and finally erupts into sinuous, multi-centred

Vladimir, Dormition Cathedral (1158, enlarged 1189): (*left*) west façade and (*right*) ground-plan (original church shaded).

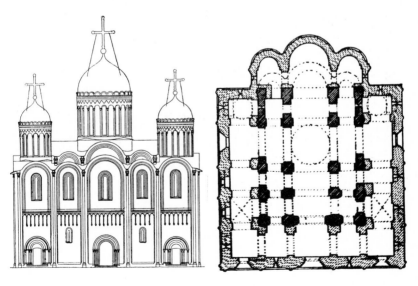

Vladimir, Cathedral of St Demetrius (1194): detail of exterior carving.

ogees at Yur'yev-Pol'sky (1230). Similarly portals and windows become more and more elaborately recessed, as do the individual panels into which the main façades are articulated; the crude pilaster-strips separating these panels become elegant engaged columns with capitals. The famous figurative carving starts with fragments discovered at the now-rebuilt palace-church of Bogolyubovo (1158); there are interesting capitals, some of them fanciful animal-heads, in the Vladimir Dormition; organized groups of figure sculpture grace the exterior wall panels of the Church on the Nerl', fill the whole upper wall to the *zakomary* on the Vladimir St Demetrius, become a richly-decorative low-relief 'tapestry' at Suzdal' (1222), which in turn creeps over the entire surface of walls, doorways and porches at Yur'yev-Pol'sky. The complex iconography – only partially Christian, employing many animal, vegetable and pagan mythical motifs (e.g. the Ascent of Alexander the Great) – is still the object of scholarly investigation. The whole church becomes a sculptured object, a sort of ivory casket in shimmering white limestone (see p. 24). It has recently been demonstrated that in all these churches the *zakomary* carried at least one more course of decorative stonework above what we see today; these courses (destroyed by weathering) rested on the now empty capitals of the engaged exterior columns, and carried the façade (for no structural reasons) up to an even more impressive height, further emphasizing the sculpturally recessed appearance of the wall panels.

Church of the Intercession on the Nerl' (1165): reconstruction of north façade (after B. Ognyov).

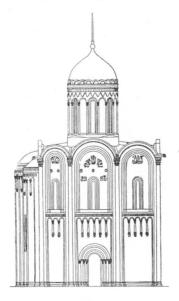

Though most late medieval Russian architecture shows awareness of the value of external decorative features, nothing like the rich carving of St Demetrius or Yur'yev-Pol'sky is known from before or since the few decades in which the Vladimir style flourished. This fact has caused much speculation about its origins, and the possible foreign influences that might have inspired it. For once no plausible Byzantine antecedents can be sought, little though Byzantine carving has been studied.[2] The once popular theory of trans-Caucasian (Georgian or Armenian) origins must be considered highly improbable; no serious stylistic or historical connexion between the sculptural decoration of trans-Caucasian churches and those of Vladimir has ever been put forward. We are left with two main possibilities: inspiration from the late Romanesque art of western Europe, or independent evolution out of the native Russian tradition.

The latter theory is not altogether absurd. Vigorous and imaginative low-relief carving, sometimes figurative, was no rarity in Kievan Russia: noteworthy are the original capitals of the Cathedral of SS Boris and Gleb in Chernigov (1120). Stone-carving was well developed in the south-western principalities of Galicia and Volhynia, from whose heritage tantalizingly little survives. Though no examples of woodcarving from so early a date have come down to us, we can be certain the art was widespread in Russia then as later, and that its techniques could conceivably be transferred to stone. Yet would Russia have independently evolved not just a manner of carving which could at any rate pass stylistically as Romanesque, but such architectural features with it as the decorative blind arcade (typical of Lombard Romanesque) and the richly-carved 'perspective' recessed portal? One is tempted to answer yes to the first two questions, no to the third; but the issue remains debatable. It raises a further problem, too: if Romanesque influence is conceded in certain aspects of this architecture, how did it arrive and for how long was it operative? One can envisage, no doubt, a team of western stonemasons with Russian, perhaps also South Slav, assistants (for the task was a huge one, quickly executed) employed on the construction of St Demetrius. But who then decorated the Church on the Nerl' thirty years earlier, or Yur'yev-Pol'sky more than thirty years later? The latter incidentally shows – with Suzdal' Cathedral – a somewhat different principle of decoration from the earlier churches, closer to what we know of early Russian popular art (both these buildings have unfortunately been much damaged and altered).

'God brought masters from all the lands to him', the chronicler tells us of Andrey Bogolyubsky's first construction of the Dormition Cathedral. 'All the lands' is usually taken to mean from outside Russia, but could

[2] Note, however, that A. Grabar has recently pointed out similarities with the thirteenth-century Byzantinesque carvings on the west front of St Mark's, Venice.

Church of the Intercession on the Nerl', near Vladimir (1165).

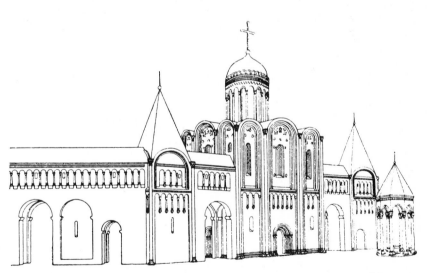

Bogolyubovo palace-complex, near Vladimir (1158): reconstruction.

25

equally well – more probably, even – refer to other Russian principalities. This may be a hint at the participation of masons from south-west Russia, where the architecture had almost certainly already absorbed some Romanesque features; the 'perspective' portal thus could have reached Vladimir through a Russian intermediary. Meanwhile these few enigmatic, amazingly perfect churches remain probably the supreme development of Old Russian architecture, to whose spirit (for all their originality) they are thoroughly true. We know something also, from visible remains, written accounts and excavations, of the lavish secular architecture which was contemporary with them: of the galleries around the Church on the Nerl' and the nearby palace-complex of Bogolyubovo, whose sight greeted travellers arriving in Vladimir by river; of the staircase tower-cum-gallery of the St Demetrius Cathedral (misguidedly demolished in the early nineteenth century) with its ogee windows; of the still-standing Golden Gate of Vladimir; of the Bogolyubovo princely palace, with its surviving tower and passageway.

The pictorial art of the age, even if we devote less attention to it than to the architecture, is impressive in quality, and much more of it survives than from the early Kievan period. To compensate for the absence of mosaics, we have the first great panel-paintings – icons – to have come down to us from Old Russia. These, in the tradition of high-Byzantine art,

'Virgin of Vladimir' icon (early twelfth century).

are monumental in character: the figures represented are large, bold and simple, with wide-open eyes, calm gestures and a general lack of individual expressiveness. But the new wind of twelfth-century art has already begun to agitate some of them. The famous Constantinopolitan icon known as the 'Virgin of Vladimir' brings the 'humane' approach into Russian icon-painting; many panels, such as the Novgorod 'Golden-haired Archangel' in the Russian Museum, Leningrad, and the 'Ustyug Annunciation', are irradiated with classical ideals of facial beauty and harmony.

The surviving fresco paintings of the age in Novgorod, Vladimir and Suzdal' are mostly fragmentary. At Vladimir one important scene has been spared: part of a 'Last Judgement' in the St Demetrius Cathedral. Specialists have unanimously seen the hand of at least one immigrant Byzantine painter here, on stylistic grounds (there is no chronicle evidence). The faces of the apostles are of a classic nobility consonant with the greatest twelfth-century Byzantine painting. Rather more of importance has been preserved (until recently at least) in Novgorod and neighbouring cities. At Pskov the Mirozhsky Monastery was decorated in the mid-twelfth century with impressive frescoes – of which so far only a few scenes have been cleaned – showing a severely linear technique. Closer to Novgorod, important paintings survive in the suburb of Arkazhi (c. 1189), and until

| Cathedral of the Nativity, Suzdal', fresco of unidentified saint (early thirteenth century). | Church of the Saviour, Nereditsa, near Novgorod: head of a prophet, fresco (1199). |

the Second World War the isolated Church of the Saviour on the Nereditsa hill (Spas na Nereditse) preserved a complete fresco-cycle, painted in 1199, which was one of the wonders of European medieval art. Two-thirds of this church's fabric was destroyed in the war, and though it has been rebuilt nearly all the paintings are lost. The style of these, and of other works of late twelfth-century Novgorod art, is severe, monumental and provincial – uningratiating yet self-assured and expressive, as if to match the rather conservative architectural taste of the city. With the loss of Nereditsa considerable importance attaches to the best (though fragmentary) comparable Novgorodian frescoes, in the church of St George at Staraya Ladoga (1160s): these are, however, closer than the former to the 'metropolitan' Byzantine manner.

Much fine applied art survives from the period, including many items of jewellery: best of all are the great doors of Suzdal' Cathedral, with panels in gold damascene-work. Ornamentation of a peculiar type termed 'teratological' (i.e. 'monstrous') is met with in various contexts (as in the Chernigov carved stone capitals mentioned above). It is of unusual interest in that it represents a late development of a very ancient north-European design-motif – an interlaced pattern featuring fantastic animal-heads – which must have welled up into 'high culture' from Russian folk sources. It was particularly important in Russian manuscript illumination up to the end of the fourteenth century.

Russia in transition: mid-thirteenth to mid-fifteenth centuries

The Tatar invasions of the fourth decade of the thirteenth century affected different parts of Russia in different ways, though in all of them cultural life suffered more or less of a shock. Some cities were irreparably devastated: Ryazan' had to be re-founded on a new site; others disappeared from the map for ever. Kiev was laid waste, and lost most of even its diminished twelfth-century importance, though it remained the ecclesiastical capital of Russia until its Metropolitan migrated to Vladimir in 1300. The cities of the north-east were pillaged, but made a quicker recovery than those of the centre and south. Finally, there were parts of Russia to which the Tatar armies did not penetrate: the extreme south-west (which soon threw in its lot with Poland–Lithuania) and the ancient north-western city-states of Novgorod and Pskov. For these the temporary disruption of trade and the burden of tribute were a severe economic setback, but they were able to preserve their cultural traditions and in some respects to strengthen their independence.

Though these events naturally affected the pattern of Russian culture and art, it would be wrong to see the *Tatarshchina* as having caused a complete dislocation in its progress, as historians sometimes imply.

Cultural life was attenuated – at least during the half-century following the invasions – yet taken as a whole this was no 'dark age'; it was a period of transition between Kiev Rus' and Muscovy, preserving strong links with the former, and developing (particularly in the years around 1400) highly interesting characteristics of its own. Inconveniently for cultural historians, no one city had such clear hegemony over Russia during this period that it could lend it a convenient name (as Kiev, Moscow, Petersburg did for other ages). Moscow's rise did not begin until the second quarter of the fourteenth century, and though with hindsight we may see its aggrandisement as inevitable, its political and cultural supremacy was vigorously challenged well into the fifteenth century by such cities as Novgorod and Tver'; we should properly not speak of 'Muscovite' Russia until the sack of Novgorod, the reconstruction of the Moscow Kremlin and the ending of the last vestiges of Tatar suzerainty in the late 1470s. In a sense we are still in Vladimir Rus': the Grand Princes' and Metropolitans' seat remained nominally the senior city until the mid-fifteenth century. For a few decades of high cultural activity on either side of 1400, however, the true intellectual centre of the country was none of the rival political capitals, but the Trinity Monastery (subsequently Lavra) recently founded by St Sergius, where the modern town of Zagorsk stands. I have elsewhere argued for the concept of a 'Sergievan' period, or subdivision, in Russian cultural history.[3]

Artistically, this period saw the magnificent development of Russian icon-painting which culminated in the work of Andrey Rublyov (see pp. 38–43); important in this connexion is the evolution, possibly on Russian soil, of the 'high' iconostasis (icon-screen in many tiers, standing in front of the altar) – the earliest known example being that of the Moscow Annunciation Cathedral (1405). It witnessed a modest but elegant and varied architecture, and fresco-paintings which equalled or surpassed those of the preceding age. For the first time sufficient material remains have been left to enable us to distinguish, albeit tentatively, the main local schools of painting. Yet our knowledge of the period is far from complete, and this central, perhaps most fully characteristic, moment in the history of Old Russian art presents us with several questions that are far from being satisfactorily answered. In particular Russia's renewed international contacts of the fourteenth century, above all with the restored Byzantine empire under the Palaeologi and with the Orthodox Slav nations of the Balkans (Serbia and Bulgaria), present important cultural–historical problems which have only been properly formulated in recent years, and which affect our conception of the intellectual life, the literature and most if not all branches of the art of this age.

[3] 'Russia's Lost Renaissance', in *Literature and Western Civilization*, III, ed. D. Daiches and A. K. Thorlby (1973), 435–68.

It is customary to date Russia's first signs of artistic recovery after the Tatar invasion to 1292, when the Church of St Nicholas on the Lipna near Novgorod was founded. Certainly it is the first building to survive to our days after the St John the Baptist (Ivanov) Monastery at Pskov (*c.* 1243): we know little about the destroyed cultural heritage of Tver', whose early rise in importance was marked by the building of its large Transfiguration Cathedral (1285). But St Nicholas on the Lipna has generally been considered to have added significance in being the first in a distinctive line of churches whose roofline originally described a delicate triple curve, rising in the middle towards a single dome. Their ground-plan is simple, with four interior columns and a single, rather large apse. This form of church, constructed at least until the late fifteenth century, is probably the most characteristic architectural pattern among the several that were developed during this period. Part of its charm is that it left considerable scope for experiment: all the surviving examples differ from each other in detail, often quite widely. Some have blind arcading under the roofline; some, broad pilaster-strips dividing the exterior into three panels, in correspondence with the curves of the façade; others, considerable exterior decoration (e.g. Novgorod, Spas na

Novgorod, St Nicholas on the Lipna (1292): west façade.

Il'ine, 1374) including patterned brickwork, window-surrounds and even carved ornament (unrelated to that of Vladimir). The shape of the trefoil curve and the proportions of the whole are freely and imaginatively treated.

Before the last war many architectural historians saw western European influence in this design, and, as so often, such a conjecture now seems groundless. Even prior to the Tatar conquest, at the beginning of the thirteenth century, the conservative Novgorod architects had begun to be infected by the twelfth-century experimental spirit. Recent investigations have proved that the little church of the Perynsky Skete at Novgorod (c. 1221) was roofed in a triple curve which is a possible ancestor of the roofline of the Lipna church, and links it with the decorative 'barrel-end' arches round the base of the drum at the earlier Yefrosin'yev Monastery, Polotsk. From as early as 1312, however, in the church known as Nikola Belyy, occasional experiments were made with a new and simpler type of roof, even over façades decorated with the trefoil curve motif: the straight-sided pitched roof, rising to a pointed gable in the middle of each façade, and thus called by the Russians *vos'miskatnaya* ('eight-sloped'). Less beguiling than the trefoil curved roofline, this type of pitched roof still has aesthetic appeal. From the sixteenth century, however, the potential of its comparative simplicity and cheapness led not only to its general adoption in new buildings, but to the wholesale reroofing of earlier monuments either in this manner, or, more often, with its yet cheaper variant, the 'four-sloped' roof; this – involving as it usually did the lopping-off or concealment of the higher parts of the façade – had aesthetically disastrous results. Only in the present century has it been understood that an earlier

Church of Volotovo, near Novgorod (1352): schematic reconstruction (after A. I. Nekrasov).

Novgorod, Church of the Transfiguration on Elijah Street (Spas na Il'ine) (1374).

31

and quite different roofline existed in such buildings: the work of restoring them has proceeded quickly in recent years (though it is still sometimes the occasion of controversy).

Not only in this Novgorod type of church has the later imposition of a pitched roof deformed the building and hindered our appreciation: all surviving specimens of the other main school of architecture, that of early Moscow, were similarly treated. Painstaking restoration in the last three decades has acquainted us with a splendid, previously under-rated series of small but finely proportioned churches, just as dependent as those of Novgorod, described above, on subtlety of outline for their main effect, and like them striving towards the centrality-pyramidality we have noted as a tendency in Kievan architecture (see pp. 11, 18), though by different means. Here for the first time *kokoshniki* (tiers of small decorative arches, named after their fanciful resemblance to a type of peasant head-dress and, as we have seen, foreshadowed already in the twelfth century) are employed in a systematic way; their typical form, and that of their arches generally, is the ogee. No influence from Gothic western Europe need be seen here: as we noted above, the earliest Russian ogees (and normally-pointed arches) predate the Tatar conquest, and are in any case differently centred from standard western patterns.

There is no reason to doubt that these churches evolved from the mainstream of Vladimir architecture; their exceptional construction in 'white stone' (limestone), which was to drop out of general use in Moscow around 1500, suggests this at once. Unfortunately the earlier buildings which would have demonstrated the link with Vladimir have all been lost, save for one or two undercrofts and foundation-storeys beneath later buildings in Moscow. Among fourteenth-century buildings a particu-larly notable example, with many domes and *kokoshniki*, must have been the cathedral at Kolomna described by the traveller Paul of Aleppo. The earliest that survives is the little Cathedral of the Dormition on the Citadel (Uspensky Sobor na Gorodke) at Zvenigorod – then the centre of a small principality just west of Moscow – which was probably built *c.* 1399. (It should be noted that the dates of all these churches have been in dispute, but the traditionally accepted dating is the most plausible.) Then come the church of the Savvino-Storozhevsky Monastery near the same town, followed by the Trinity Cathedral at St Sergius' Monastery, and – perhaps the finest of the series – the Andronikov Monastery in Moscow (constructed some time between 1410 and 1427; today the oldest standing building in the city). There is reason to believe that the great Andrey Rublyov had a hand in the original decoration of all these churches; he probably helped actually to design that of the Andronikov Monastery. The original form of all these buildings has now been estab-lished with a reasonable degree of certainty. They made restrained but effective use of *kokoshniki*, an upper tier of which was arranged in an octagon around the base of the drum. If one is to believe the recent reconstruction by N. N. Voronin, a direct forebear of this pattern must have been the early thirteenth-century church at Yur'yev-Pol'sky. Like the *zakomary* of the Vladimir group of churches, the *kokoshniki* of the Zvenigorod churches and the Andronikov Monastery rose in a 'false façade' above the true roofline, betraying their decorative rather than constructional function. The external division of the façades by pilasters no longer fully corresponds with the internal structure.[4] These small innovations all point the way to future developments. Meanwhile a lengthy internecine struggle (marking in important respects the end of a whole historical period) held up further artistic activity in Muscovy until the later part of the fifteenth century.

Little survives of the contemporary architecture elsewhere in Russia. The south-western lands, after the Tatar invasions, take a path which was to lead them away from the mainstream of Russian culture for several centuries, during which the Ukrainian and White Russian languages differentiate themselves from Great Russian. From the period under consideration their chief remaining monuments are of defensive architecture (e.g. the fortress at Lutsk, thirteenth and fourteenth centuries).

Zvenigorod, Dormition Cathedral (*c.* 1399): reconstruction of north façade.   Zagorsk, Trinity Cathedral of St Sergius Monastery (1422).

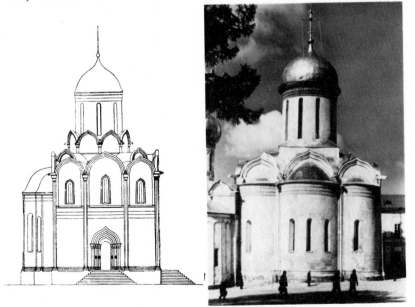

[4] Suzdal' Cathedral of the Nativity (1230) to some extent anticipates this development.

33

Soon direct influences from Gothic (and in the sixteenth-century Renaissance) western Europe and Balkan influences through Moldavia turn the art of these regions into what might best be described as a 'central European' direction.

Novgorod, similarly placed in close commercial contact with the rest of Europe, shows on the other hand few demonstrable artistic consequences of this fact at any stage in its history. If there was any influence, it was mainly in a reverse direction: Novgorod artists may have painted certain western churches, such as that of Gärde on Gotland, Sweden. Individual items – even the massive twelfth-century bronze doors of the Novgorod Sophia, most of whose panels were executed in Magdeburg – had of course found their way in from the west, as they did to other parts of Russia; and a single Gothic-vaulted chamber, the Granovitaya Palata of the Archbishop's Palace, was built by German and Russian masters in 1433. This was part of the considerable constructional and restoring activity of the great Archbishop Euthymius, the last major statesman of the independent city before 'Lord Novgorod the Great' was sacked by the armies of Moscow in 1478 and its cultural achievements were systematically taken over or destroyed. It demonstrates that large public buildings were now being constructed (previously churches acted as secular, as well as sacred meeting places). So, in the Novgorod and Pskov lands, were massive stone fortifications: the walls of Kopor'ye probably date from Euthymius' time, and bear features which relate them closely, perhaps significantly, to castles in the south Slavonic countries (Ohrid, Belgrade).

Novgorod and Pskov, in fact, comparatively unreceptive to the artistic developments in the west, were at least from the beginning of the fourteenth century notably sensitive to the new trends which were affecting the pictorial art of Byzantium and the Balkans. A few instances of direct cultural contact can be demonstrated: examples are the copying of Serbian miniatures in the 1360s, apparent 'Serbisms' in the inscriptions and style of one at least of the masters at work on the fresco cycle in the church of Kovalyovo (1380), the fine 'feast-day' icons of the Novgorod Sophia (early fourteenth century), above all the activity of Theophanes the Greek. But, more broadly, the spirit of Novgorodian art – at least from the time of the 'Vasil'yev Gates' (1336), subsequently installed by Ivan the Terrible at Aleksandrov, perhaps from as early as St Nicholas on the Lipna or the Snetogorsk Monastery at Pskov (supposedly 1313) – responded to the stylistic methods of the so-called 'Palaeologan Renaissance'.

The history of the Palaeologan style is complicated, but it can be characterized in general terms as a development of twelfth/thirteenth-century tendencies emphasizing striking effects of colour, light and movement, heightened emotionalism, classically-based modelling and draughtsmanship, multi-figured, often small-scale scenes and some modification (usually in the direction of complexity) of traditional iconography. Its apparent though elusive connexions with early Renaissance painting in the west have been much discussed. D. S. Likhachev has convincingly proposed the notion of an eastern pre- (rather than 'proto-') Renaissance movement, to embrace phenomena of this period not only in the spheres of art and literature, but also intellectual life (notably the 'Hesychast' mystical current within the Orthodox Church – whose effect would appear to be reflected in the newly-dramatic artistic representation of scenes such as the Transfiguration). V. N. Lazarev, while disputing some of Likhachev's main conclusions, has made a valuable contribution in defining two main stages of Palaeologan art: a 'painterly' phase, producing the chief master-pieces of the period, and a 'linear' manner – often dry and academic – which replaced it in the mid-fourteenth century: first in Byzantium, more gradually at the periphery. This observation, incidentally, displaces Millet's once widely-held theory of supposed 'Cretan' and 'Macedonian' schools of Orthodox art.

For Byzantium the Palaeologan period can be exactly measured: from the recapture of Constantinople from the Latins in 1261 to its fall in 1453. In Russia the periodization is unavoidably less definite, but it was during much the same time-span that Russian painting experienced its greatest flowering. Russia's contribution to Palaeologan art – sometimes overlooked by Byzantinists – was in fact very considerable, and generally avoided the twin potential dangers of oversophistication and dryness. Lazarev's 'linear' phase is actually the stage at which the most character-istically Russian elements become deeply embedded in its art. Rublyov himself is one of the early representatives of this manner (which suggests that Lazarev's generally hostile characterization of late-Palaeologan painting deserves some modification). But before the general change to a linear approach, the 'painterly' Palaeologan style – the style of the Kariye Cami in Constantinople, of the great Ohrid icons and of many other major works – had a lengthy, if individualistic, development on Russian soil. It was refined and perpetuated by the example of the most famous Greek émigré artist in medieval Russia, perhaps the finest Byzan-tine painter whose name has come down to us, Theophanes the Greek (Feofan Grek).

We know more about Theophanes than the laconic chronicle entries recording some of his commissions, thanks to a remarkable fragment of a letter from one Epiphanius – who is almost certainly identical with Epiphanius 'The Wise' (*Premudryy*), biographer of St Sergius and the greatest Russian writer of the age – to a friend Kirill. Epiphanius answers his friend's enquiry about the origin of a certain miniature illumination with detailed reminiscences of Theophanes, whom he knew personally.

35

He mentions the Byzantine and Russian towns where Theophanes had worked, and describes his manner of painting:

> While he delineated and painted all these things no one ever saw him looking at models as some of our painters do who, being filled with doubt, constantly [peer at] them casting their eyes hither and thither, and instead of painting with colours they gaze at the models as often as they need to. He, however, seemed to be painting with his hands, while his feet moved without rest, his tongue conversed with visitors, his mind dwelled on something lofty and wise, and his rational eyes contemplated that beauty which is rational.[5]

We have so little first-hand information about methods of work and attitudes towards it of Russian and Byzantine painters that Epiphanius' letter is a uniquely valuable document. He also gives us an account of Theophanes' and his own activity as miniaturists.

Theophanes' style of painting has to be judged on the basis of fragmentary frescoes in a single church, the only ones to survive in the very many he so decorated: the Church of the Transfiguration on Elijah Street (Spas na Il'ine, painted 1378) in Novgorod. He can also be considered to

Theophanes the Greek, 'Old Testament Trinity' fresco, Church of the Transfiguration on Elijah Street, Novgorod (1378).

[5] Translated by Cyril Mango, in *The Art of the Byzantine Empire, 312–1453* (Englewood Cliffs, N J., 1972). The words 'peer at' are my alteration.

have painted some of the icons that stand in the Annunciation Cathedral of the Moscow Kremlin. The several other works – frescoes, icons and miniatures – attributed to him by enthusiasts at various times up to the present must all, with reluctance, be attributed to imitators, or perhaps in some cases to his workshop. As Epiphanius might lead us to expect, Theophanes' painting is characterized by a freedom and brio not easily matched elsewhere in the art of the time, eastern or western. With a starkly limited range of colour he makes dramatic use of highlights (applied in impressionistic white daubs): this is not precisely chiaroscuro, since (as always in Byzantine art) there is no single source of light and no true shadowing. The stern, possessed faces of his saints have suggested to some commentators that their creator was at least a sympathizer with prevalent dualistic heresy. This is improbable: but his art may well have been affected by current Orthodox mysticism directly or indirectly. The Annunciation Cathedral icons, if they are from his brush (and it is hard to doubt the attribution in the case of the striking, dark-clad Virgin, and two or three others), are more static and stylistically· restrained than the Novgorod frescoes, as indeed befits the medium.

Two major churches in Novgorod have – or had until the complete destruction of one of them in the Second World War – frescoes showing the influence of Theophanes: St Theodore Stratelates (much faded) and the Church of the Dormition at Volotovo. In the latter there is no slavish imitation: Theophanes' free and intense example had inspired the unknown Russian artists to a decorative ensemble of unequalled virtuosity, expressive and jagged in style, straining the language of medieval mural painting to its limit. The cycle was remarkably complete and well preserved; its destruction was as great a loss as that of Nereditsa, perhaps greater. Also following the general manner of Theophanes are three or four icons now in the Tret'yakov Gallery, Moscow: notably the large, brilliantly-coloured and dramatic 'Pereyaslavl' Transfiguration', and a stark Dormition.

To juxtapose Theophanes with his younger, Russian, colleague Andrey Rublyov is to appreciate the free-ranging dynamic possibilities of Russian culture in the years around 1400. Both belong not just to the broad tradition of Byzantine Orthodox art, but specifically to the narrower field of the art of Russia: Theophanes, like certain much later immigrants who were to make their second home in Russia, not only made his idiosyncratic contribution to its culture, but himself worked within its spirit and was sensitive to some of its earlier achievements. (A. Grabar and others have pointed out interesting anticipations of Theophanes' manner in the early fourteenth-century Snetogorsk Monastery frescoes.) Yet, within these limits, we can scarcely imagine two painters as different as Theophanes and Rublyov. It is not simply that Theophanes' techniques basically (and belatedly) belong to the 'painterly' Palaeologan manner, and Rublyov's to the 'linear', as described above. Their entire concepts of art differ: the calm spaciousness, curvilinear rhythms and air of gentleness in Rublyov's work contrast fundamentally with Theophanes' nervous dynamism of form and emotional extremism. To see in Rublyov Theophanes' pupil, as some art-historians have done, is quite implausible. Rather we should place his formation as an artist in the central Russia

Moscow, Annunciation Cathedral in the Kremlin (1484, central tiers of iconostasis 1405).

(Moscow or the Trinity Monastery) of the 1390s, among 'progressive', Graecophile circles, and perhaps (following Lazarev's suggestion) under the tutelage of Prokhor from Gorodets, a colleague of Theophanes and Rublyov in the decoration of the Annunciation Cathedral, and described as *starets* (the 'elder') by the chronicler. This does not of course mean that Rublyov need have remained indifferent to Theophanes' example or even to individual aspects of his artistic technique; but he was evidently a mature painter, with his own artistic vision, before he came into contact with Theophanes.

Our knowledge of the fourteenth-century pictorial art of central Russia that bore such remarkable fruit in Rublyov's work is inadequate, and primarily based on a small number of early Muscovite icons; no relevant frescoes have been discovered. With the Tatar invasions, the capture of Constantinople by the armies of the Fourth Crusade (1204), and the consequent slackening of Russia's international contacts, icon-painting in both the Novgorod and the former Vladimir lands had witnessed a strengthening of provincial and even folk characteristics alongside a generally more plastic and unclassical treatment of the traditionally monumental poses we observed in Kievan art. Moscow painting before Rublyov – including the icons probably attributable to Prokhor among those in the Annunciation Cathedral – shows instances of clumsiness and naïveté, but also a certain undemonstrative grace and even suavity, with a characteristically soft, almost feminine depiction of saints and angels (though certain other icons of around 1400 reflect the impact of Theophanes' activity in Moscow). The earliest paintings that have been conjecturally attributed to Rublyov – fragmentary frescoes in the Dormition Cathedral (*c.* 1399) at Zvenigorod – accord with the Moscow tradition, without yet displaying his mature mastery; nor is this mastery yet completely manifest in his probable contributions to the Moscow Annunciation Cathedral iconostasis of 1405, when his name is first mentioned in the chronicles. Three years later, however, he was creating some of his finest work. The chronicles record, under 1408, his participation in the redecoration of the great Dormition Cathedral in Vladimir, together with his lifelong friend Daniil Chornyy. Some of their frescoes – chiefly part of an extensive 'Last Judgement' – have survived, though patchy and faded, to the present. So, by great good fortune, has much of the huge iconostasis, sold off in the eighteenth century to the parishioners of a distant village.

The 'Last Judgement' in the Vladimir Dormition includes the scenes of Paradise, but those of Hell have been lost. This may help to condition, but does not fully account for, our sense of a gentleness, even on occasion a playfulness, that irradiates and transforms the basic gravity of the subject-matter. In this respect it is interesting to compare a scene such as the Entry

39

of the Righteous into Paradise, complete with trumpeting angels, with its treatment more than 200 years earlier in the neighbouring frescoes of St Demetrius. Rublyov's harmonious grouping of figures, his tendency towards circularity of basic forms (particularly noticeable in his simply-drafted, serious yet cheerful, almost peasant-like faces) show the hallmarks of his manner immediately. In most of the scenes and individual figures there is no difficulty in distinguishing between his approach and a more archaic, angular style of painting which we can reasonably guess to be Daniil's. Attribution of the icons is harder: they are better preserved, but plainer and more laconically treated. The immense figures (over 3 metres high) of the lower range demand to be seen from a distance and in the right setting, which today is alas impossible. Assistants probably had a large part in their execution.

Rublyov's further activity, as recorded in near-contemporary sources, consisted in the decoration of the new cathedrals of the two great monasteries in which he had lived: St Sergius' Trinity Lavra and the Andronikov Monastery in Moscow, where he died on 29 January 1430 'at a great age' (he was probably born in the later 1360s). Both commissions date from the late 1420s. Within the Andronikov Monastery only insignificant scraps of fresco survive; yet there is an early source from which one may deduce

Andrey Rublyov, angel from the 'Last Judgement' fresco (1408), Vladimir, Dormition Cathedral.

Archangel Michael icon from Zvenigorod, attributed to A. Rublyov (early fifteenth century).

Andrey Rublyov, icon of the 'Old Testament Trinity' (1410s or 1420s).

that he designed the cathedral itself, the finest of the early Muscovite buildings. This is not implausible (one thinks of Giotto's Campanile in Florence); if so this is Rublyov's last surviving work, and it is appropriate that the monastery should now house the museum named after him. The Trinity Cathedral at the Lavra was built in 1423–4, and decorated in a hurry (before 1427) by Rublyov, his old colleague and close friend Daniil, and 'certain others' – in fact a large team working in a variety of recognizable manners, as we can see from the surviving iconostasis. Attribution of any of these icons to Rublyov himself is problematical, since followers of his style were undoubtedly among his team. But the figure of St Paul and two or three more would seem to be by him (as also of course was the 'Old Testament Trinity' – see below). Old age and haste no doubt limited his contribution.

Though we have no record of what Rublyov painted in the 1410s and early 1420s, there is reason to believe that this may have been the finest period of his achievement. It is almost certain that he worked again for Prince Yury of Zvenigorod; some fragmentarily preserved saints decorating the stone altar-rail in the church of the Savvino-Storozhevsky Monastery (of uncertain date) are reasonably attributed by Lazarev and others to him. But more important are three great icons, from the central part of a Deesis, which were discovered in celebrated circumstances (under a pile of firewood) at Zvenigorod in 1918. No finer linked group, it may reasonably be asserted, survives anywhere in the world. Much of the paintwork has been destroyed or damaged (particularly on the central Saviour), but the faces are in good condition, and the glowing colour of the St Paul and in particular the Archangel Michael need to be seen to be believed. St Michael – represented elsewhere in Orthodox art in a wide variety of manners ranging from the ferocious to the effete – is imbued with a totally Rublyovian spirit: classically grave, serene, contemplative and tender. The closeness of this, and of the haunting image of the Saviour, to Rublyov's attested work is such as to leave the attribution in little doubt. But it is uncertain where these great half-figure icons were intended to stand: neither of the two small Zvenigorod cathedrals could easily have accommodated a full Deesis range of such dimensions.

Rublyov's most celebrated work, the 'Old Testament Trinity' icon from the Trinity Monastery, may also date from these intermediate years: it has much in common, both in spirit and execution, with the Zvenigorod St Michael. It is the only work which a long-standing and apparently unbroken tradition connects with Rublyov, and it was rightly taken as a starting-point in the earlier part of this century for the establishment of his canon. It was painted, according to a seventeenth-century source, in memory of St Sergius. It represents the Trinity, to whom Sergius dedicated himself and his monastery, in the manner customary in the Orthodox world: through the image of the three strangers welcomed and feasted by Abraham under the oak of Mamre (Genesis 18). To a degree unmatched in any large-scale representation of this subject before or since, Rublyov reduces inessentials: not only the equipment of the meal, but the very figures of Abraham and Sarah have been eliminated from the normal iconography, leaving a single stark chalice about which the whole composition revolves. But, like much great art, this picture succeeds in being fundamentally simple and resonant with implications at the same time. It would be inappropriate to attempt here an analysis, necessarily lengthy, of the symbolic, historical and spiritual significance of the Trinity icon; let it suffice to mention two or three formal characteristics that point towards it. Most immediately noticeable of these are probably the circularity of the group of figures, the harmonious rhythm of their postures, their unity-in-diversity. More subtle and just as important is the rhythm of colours: the brilliant deep sky-blue (from lapis lazuli) which is seen on each figure; the dominating splash of blood red on the sleeve of the central angel which reappears in the chalice (though in contemplating the colour harmony we must remember that some of the paint-surface, particularly in the background, is worn or damaged). Unobtrusive use of Byzantine 'reverse perspective' renders the scene both incorporeal and self-sufficient. The classical *gravitas* of the faces and gestures suggests deep but restrained emotion, indicating to many commentators the mingled expression of brotherhood and suffering.

One or two other works are attributed on reasonable grounds to Rublyov's brush by modern scholars; but in general the tendency has been (as with Theophanes) to cut down, rather than extend, the canon of authenticity as Rublyov's distinguishing qualities have come to be better appreciated. Consideration of these two great painters may lead us to a consideration of the role of the individual in a medieval culture which did not consciously strive for individuality, and to a recognition of the new role of personality in this 'pre-Renaissance' age. But we should not be tempted by our knowledge of a few outstanding names to discount the contribution of the anonymous artists who helped to make this the outstanding age of icon-painting both in achievement and variety. In particular a remarkably characteristic, but not yet stereotyped style of painting is forged in Novgorod, and reaches its culmination around the mid-fifteenth century. In it a strong degree of linear stylization has not yet ousted gracefulness, an infusion of folk elements has not yet led to anti-classical deformation, patches of strong, clear colour (notably the brilliant vermilion sometimes called 'Novgorod red') have not upset harmony and subtlety. In their strong yet delicate simplicity, fifteenth-century Novgorod icons such as the Tret'yakov Gallery 'Entombment' and 'St George' break down the barriers between the popular and the

Novgorod, icon of the 'Old Testament Trinity' (fifteenth century).

sophisticated in a characteristic, admirably Russian way. Among anonymous central Russian painters a rhythmic daring that outstrips Rublyov is shown, for example, by one of the masters of the Trinity Monastery iconostasis who painted 'The Women at the Tomb'. The most important of the lesser schools of painting, which must have grown up in all the main cities, was doubtless that of Pskov (an independent city-state since 1348), with its typical facial type and dark tones, particularly a characteristic green; a small number of outstanding icons are attributable to Moscow's great rival-city, Tver'.

The minor arts of this period have left us an abundance of material in comparison with the Kievan age. We have the first surviving wooden sculpture: statues of saints and carved icons, among which a small triptych (1456) by the master Amvrosy at Zagorsk is outstanding. The excellent examples of silver, enamel and ivory work are too numerous to mention; but it is worth noting the small round pendant-icons, often representing the 'Old Testament Trinity', whose forms probably in some measure inspired Rublyov's large panel, and some of which in turn were subsequently influenced by it. A few carved stone crosses survive, notably the fine example from Borovichi, near Novgorod (*c.* 1300). But the most outstanding of the lesser arts at this time was manuscript illumination. The rather uncouth but vigorous 'teratological' style of ornament gave way around 1400 to drier 'geometrical' forms thought by scholars to have reached Russia from the Balkans. At the moment of transition, however, a small number of illustrated manuscripts neither in the one style nor the

Icon of the Archangel Michael, Moscow school (early fifteenth century), formerly attributed to A. Rublyov.

'The Women at the Tomb' icon, Trinity Cathedral, Zagorsk (mid-fifteenth century).

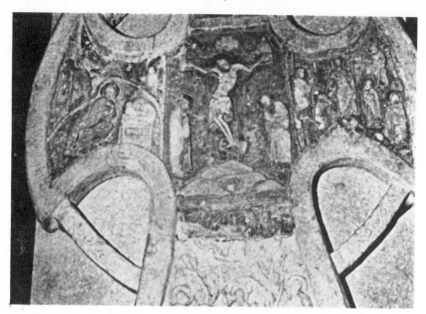

Carved stone cross from Borovichi (early fourteenth century): detail.

Angel representing St Matthew, from the Khitrovo Gospel, circle of Andrey
Rublyov (late fourteenth or early fifteenth century).

46

other were produced; rather they seem to represent a creative development of middle-Byzantine traditions. Their vigorous and imaginative techniques, their refinement and polish make them Russia's finest contribution to this art form. They include the so-called Khitrovo, Morozov, Koshka and Andronikov Monastery Gospels; also notable, in a different manner, is the Kiev Psalter (1397). The genesis and interrelationships of the four sets of gospels have been often but inconclusively studied; the workshops of both Theophanes the Greek and Rublyov have variously been put forward as their place of origin. Particularly striking are the symbolized evangelists in the Khitrovo Gospel, and the splendidly realistic, cheerful and inventive animal-figures in the Khitrovo and the Morozov manuscripts – not easily paralleled in contemporary Orthodox art, unless by the remarkable, much-faded scene 'The Earth and Sea deliver up their Dead' in Rublyov's Vladimir frescoes of 1408.

Muscovy: late fifteenth century to the end of the seventeenth century

The centralized, autocratic Muscovite state, self-styled heir to Rome and Constantinople, was established by Ivan III in the last quarter of the fifteenth century, and by 1510 (with the suppression of the independence of Pskov) had eliminated any possibility of separate political or cultural development in the Great Russian lands. Moscow became by far the most important centre of artistic and architectural activity, its tsars the dominant patrons.

From this period date most of the picturesque churches, small and large, which punctuate Russia's landscape and give colour to its cities; so do the vast majority of icons and other *objets d'art* that have survived from Old Russia, including all, or virtually all, those that have found their way abroad. Within the period buildings and icons from the middle and later seventeenth century predominate. All this has tended to colour, perhaps detrimentally, popular notions of Old Russian artistic culture in the west and (at least until the early twentieth century) within Russia itself. When Russia's early painting has seemed hieratic, flat, stereotyped, or its architecture over-ornate and ill-proportioned, Muscovy has been responsible.

There is more to the art of the Muscovite period than that, however. Above all there is a variety of exploration and experiment – some of it misconceived, much of it crudely realized, but adding up to a worthwhile contribution to the history of European art, and demonstrating the continued dynamic potential within the culture of the Orthodox world even in decline. For this period does represent a decline aesthetically from the great days of Kiev, Vladimir, Novgorod and early Moscow, and it would be wrong to ignore this fact. The achievements of an earlier age are now institutionalized and slowly sapped of their vigour: this applies equally to Rublyov's visionary painting, Epiphanius' expressive literary style, or SS Sergius' and Stephen of Perm''s religious and intellectual mission. Much of what is new and forward-looking in Muscovite art is the result of revivification through folk-art, or chance moments of contact with the west. Such contacts did not of course lead yet to absorption into a western cultural system, since the full Renaissance did not come to Russia. Why this should be so is a problem whose investigation has scarcely begun; undoubtedly the fall of Byzantium, cultural intermediary between Russia and Europe, to the Turks in 1453 played some part. At least it should be said that the decline in artistic quality was not as rapid and widespread as it was in the Balkans in the seventeenth century, and that the last phase of Old Russian art – the later seventeenth century – unexpectedly shows a vitality unmatched since the days of Rublyov.

This leads us to consider what subdivisions might be contemplated within this long and heterogeneous period. The most obvious one would be between the sixteenth century and the seventeenth, if we observe the

Yur'yev-Pol'sky, Vladimir region, St George's Cathedral (1230, rebuilt by V. Yermolin for Ivan III, 1471).

historical caesura of the 'Time of the Troubles'. A subtler but perhaps
profounder difference sets off the last quarter of the seventeenth century –
the early part of the Russian Baroque age – from all that went before.
In some respects the reign of Ivan the Terrible (1533–84) marks the
beginning of a new stage. But since certain basic characteristics run
through the whole period, and since painting and architecture develop
in a rather less synchronized way than earlier, it seems wise to treat
Muscovite Russia as a single entity as far as artistic periodization is
concerned.

In Russian culture of the fifteenth century a conscious antiquarianism
can be observed: it was marked, in its earlier stage, by a potentially Renaissance nostalgia for a pre-Tatar age of glory and harmony, later by a
proud desire to outdo past achievements. Old buildings were restored;
Ivan III ordered a (somewhat clumsy) rebuilding which has preserved
for us the precious sculpted church of Yur'yev-Pol'sky. It is scarcely
surprising therefore that when Ivan wished to ornament his Kremlin
with a suitably large cathedral and (after a tragi-comic episode involving
incompetent Moscow masons and the summoning of an investigatory
commission of builders from Pskov) brought in an Italian engineer to
tackle the job, he made his immigrant employee study the masterpieces
of early Russian architecture. Aristotele Fioravanti managed his task
well in the circumstances: he produced a tall and imposing building in
'white stone' and brick, a passable if regularized Old Russian pastiche
with nothing recognizably Italian about it. Only when it is compared with

Moscow Kremlin, Dormition Cathedral (1475): south façade.

49

its prototype in Vladimir does the Moscow Dormition Cathedral (1475) disappoint, in its general stylelessness and the huddled effect of its five big domes. But it has a fine airy interior (upheld on four slim round piers) containing parts of its original frescoed décor of the 1480s, a collection of notable icons and the remarkable carved-wood throne of Ivan the Terrible (1551).

Ivan III's Dormition Cathedral was only one item in a broad programme of building that was soon to give the Moscow Kremlin (and in particular its Cathedral Square) something like the form we see today. More Italians were brought in to design a variety of structures: the Faceted Palace (Granovitaya Palata, 1487), an improbable small palazzo whose fenestration was remodelled in the seventeenth century; the stout Kremlin walls with their north-Italian swallowtail battlements – though not yet their

Moscow Kremlin, Dormition Cathedral; throne of Ivan the terrible, bottom right.

tower-superstructures; the lower stages of the fine belfry Ivan Velikiy ('Big John', generally but wrongly called 'Belfry of Ivan the Great', 1505, completed by Russians in 1600); lastly, and most important, the Cathedral of the Archangel Michael. This, designed by the architect Alevisio Novi in 1505, daringly integrates high-Renaissance articulation and decorative detail (the famous scallop-shells in the *zakomary*, heavy cornices, stuccoed relief) with the traditional four-column cross-in-square plan. The unex-

Moscow Kremlin, Archangel Cathedral, by A. Novi (1505).

51

pectedly satisfying result had more effect on Russian architecture than any of the Italians' other innovations, perhaps because the Archangel Cathedral manages to seem both strikingly innovatory and basically within the traditions of former Russian architecture at the same time.

The jewel of the Cathedral Square, however, is none of these buildings, but the comparatively small (though originally three-domed) Annunciation Cathedral, built by Ivan's team of Pskov builders in 1484 to replace the church decorated by Theophanes, Prokhor and Rublyov, whose iconostasis was evidently transferred to the new structure. It stands on the first building's solid white-stone crypt; its rather rambling galleries and extra domes are later additions. Its gilded roof makes subtle play with stepped *zakomary*; inside it boasts not only the great iconostasis, but a beautiful floor of semi-precious stones, and damascene-panelled doors. The Pskov team had, in fact, a busy and in some ways puzzling sojourn in Moscow during the 1470s and 1480s. Their first work was the Church of the Holy Spirit (1476) in the Trinity Monastery, which surprisingly houses an open bell-tower in the drum of its single dome. This,

Church at Yurkino, Moscow province (early sixteenth century): reconstruction of south façade.

like the other small but elegant churches they built, was constructed in
brick – Pskov architecture had known, so far as we can tell, only stone –
and in a manner somewhat closer to the early Muscovite tradition of
architecture than to that of their native city (a few of whose characteristic
decorative elements are, however, seen in the ornamental friezes). In
Pskov itself, as in Novgorod, small churches in forms developed during
the previous age were still constructed in the sixteenth century; their
chief novelty lies not (as used to be thought) in their characteristic column-
less interior plan, but in their picturesque detached bell-towers. Small
churches built about 1500 in and around Moscow itself (St Tryphon-
in-Naprudnoye; the Conception of St Anne at Yurkino) combine the
general appearance of early Muscovite architecture discussed above
with a less inventive roofline and two features formerly characteristic of
Novgorod: the triple-curved façade and a single, large apse. *Kokoshniki*,
reduced in size and no longer even giving the illusion of constructive
purpose, are by now simply an applied decorative feature: they may be
round-headed, pointed, ogee-shaped or triangular. Though many small
churches built in this period are still attractive in outline, a tendency
towards dumpiness and disproportion grows from the early sixteenth
century.

Nothing in all this prepares us for the remarkable, even bizarre, events
that were to take place in Russian architecture from 1530 to the 1550s.
In the former year Vasily III, probably to celebrate the birth of a long-

Kolomenskoye, Church of the Ascension (1532): (*left*) east façade and (*right*)
ground-plan.

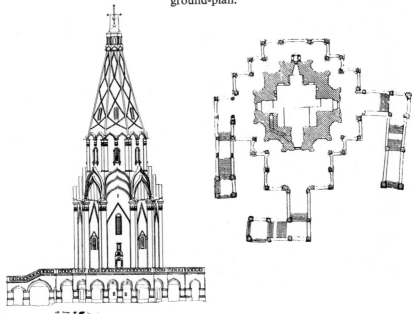

awaited son (the future Ivan the Terrible), founded a church on his private estate of Kolomenskoye near Moscow which astonished his contemporaries by its beauty, and may still astonish us today: it rises from a low but massive galleried base in a single tall brick spire or 'tent' (*shatyor*), with detail in white stone. Only a mere hint of rounding at the top gives a suggestion of the traditional, indeed canonical dome. Long suspicions that this form had been adapted from the traditional wooden architecture of Russia were confirmed by Tikhomirov's discovery (1941) in a little-known chronicle of a reference to its construction 'in the wooden manner' (*na derevyannoye delo*). Other churches (at whose appearance we can only guess) are known to have been built of wood after the manner of brick: so we have positive evidence of the cross-fertilization, prima facie rather improbable, between these two quite disparate media of construction; the possibility of the influence of wooden architecture on earlier Russian stone building (perhaps, e.g., in the development of *kokoshniki*) can no longer be dismissed out of hand. Naturally, since brick lacks the strength-to-lightness ratio of wood, the walls of such a 'tent-church' – buttressed only by decorative pilasters – had to be extraordinarily solid, the interior space very small. For the first time in

Kolomenskoye, Church of the Ascension (1532).

D'yakovo, near Moscow, Church of St John the Baptist (probably 1547): west façade.

Russian church design,[6] the Church of the Ascension at Kolomenskoye and its successors break decisively, not just with the external forms of traditional architecture (after all, this type can be regarded as an end-product of that striving towards pyramidality and centrality which we have observed so often before), but also with the incredibly tenacious Byzantine cross-in-square ground plan; of the two, this was perhaps the greater revolution.

The next in the series of churches that experiment with the 'tower' or 'spire' shape was built at D'yakovo, within sight of Kolomenskoye, c. 1547. Its brutal forms are even more surprising, though a good deal less ingratiating, than those of its predecessor. As in the Kremlin Archangel Cathedral, certain western Renaissance features (e.g. sunken rectangular wall-panels) are oddly combined with Russian detail, and in its very conception there may be a distorted echo of Renaissance designs. D'yakovo might be considered an experiment without issue, were it not that reminiscences of its silhouette seem to have been combined with the spire principle of Kolomenskoye in the genesis of the greatest, most complex and *outré* of sixteenth-century Russian buildings, built in 1555–60 on Red Square outside the Kremlin walls of Moscow: the Church of the Intercession 'on the Ditch' (Pokrov na Rvu), which became popularly known as the Cathedral of Basil the Blessed, or 'St Basil's'.

This is one of the world's great buildings, about which legends collect. Founded to commemorate Ivan the Terrible's capture of Kazan', it must

Moscow, Church of the Intercession ('St Basil's', 1555): (*left*) plan at first floor level and (*right*) west façade.

[6] Recent research indicates a possible forerunner to Kolomenskoye, however: the brick spire above the refectory of the Spassky Monastery at Suzdal' (1520s).

55

owe much of its whimsicality to the monarch's fantasy; he supposedly –
for such myths are as old as architecture itself – blinded its Russian builders,
Barma and Postnik, so as to prevent their designing anything to surpass it
(some historians consider Barma/Postnik one and the same person). For
all the initial irregularity of its appearance, the church is built to a symmetrical, if rather perverse, plan: eight chapels, alternately round and
angular, are ranged about a central core-church; all have their own
dedications, each stands separate from the others (hence the curious corridors and spaces inside the building), and each is crowned by a domed
tower – with a tall *shatyor* in the centre. Surface decoration – tiers of deformed *kokoshniki*, bright polychrome paintwork – has been obsessively
applied to every part of the outer surface, even to the skin of the onion
domes; inside, a splendid jungle of painted foliage creeps over the walls and
corridors. The outside staircases (later galleried), whereby the churches
are reached, form an integrated element of the whole; the foundation-
storey below has a fortress-like solidity that unexpectedly contradicts the
immaterial vision of those improbable towers. It is ironic that this
cathedral, the like of which was never seen in Old Russian architecture
before or since, has come to typify this architecture in the minds of many
non-Russians. The wild perversity of its detail can provoke understandable
revulsion; yet few who have seen its splendidly-grouped domes appearing
to float above the gently sloping expanses of Red Square can have withheld
their astonished admiration.

Tent-churches, simple or composite, continued to be built throughout
the sixteenth and the first half of the seventeenth centuries; the form of the
shatyor becomes the normal roofing for porches and bell-towers. Such

Moscow, Red Square. *Left to right:* Church of the Intercession or 'St Basil's'
(Barma and Postnik, 1555); Spassky Gate (Christopher Galloway, 1625 – upper
parts); Kremlin walls (Ruffo, Solario *et al.*, 1485 onwards); Lenin Mausoleum
(A. V. Shchusev, 1929); former Senate building (M. F. Kazakov, 1776).

buildings range from the simplest village examples – a stumpy pyramid on a cube (Prusy, south of Moscow) – to the elegant triple spires of the Divnaya ('Marvellous') Church at Uglich, and to the profusion of slim, calculatedly irregular and purely decorative *flèches* crowning the remarkable Church of the Nativity in Putinki, Moscow (1649). The form appears to have faded out of general use when the Patriarch Nikon, objecting to uncanonical distortions of Orthodox practice, prescribed the traditional five-domed type. Yet examples (e.g. Annino, near Ruza) are found from as late as the 'Moscow Baroque' age, and ironically the great domed rotunda of Nikon's own monastery of New Jerusalem at Istra in the Moscow region (1656; remodelled in the eighteenth century, destroyed in the last war) must have been one of the most daring developments of the tent principle.

Surviving examples of tent-churches are not very numerous; though we know (if only from early sketches of villages and towns) that the type was widespread, it never ousted more conservative patterns of church architecture, which themselves indeed were subject to innovatory tendencies – during the seventeenth century in particular. A type of large, plain, official church, obviously following (if debasing) the example of the Moscow Dormition Cathedral, continued to be built frequently in cities and important monasteries. It need not detain us. More interesting are the small churches, now without interior columns – the development of the vaulting system needed for this was particularly associated with Pskov – weighed down though they may sometimes appear with their load of *kokoshniki* (Rubtsovo, 1619; the Donskoy Monastery 'Old'

New Jerusalem, Moscow province, Ascension Cathedral (1656, dome reconstructed in 1750s): cross-section.

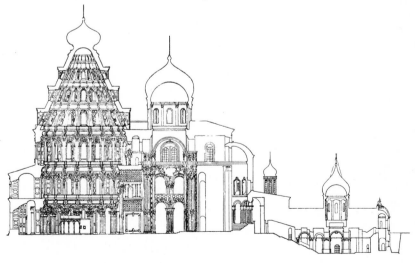

Cathedral, 1591). The drum and dome often dwindle to a decorative adjunct, no longer functionally connected with the interior. Middle-sized churches remain rather conservative in the sixteenth and early seventeenth centuries, and often retain much simple grace (the cathedral at Dmitrov; Vyazyomy). In the mid-seventeenth century they blossom into highly decorative, even sumptuous forms, particularly in Moscow and the newly-prosperous trading city of Yaroslavl' (the Church of the Trinity in Nikitniki, Moscow, 1634, may serve as a single example of the very many that survive). Virtuoso use of patterned brickwork and decorative ceramic are characteristic of such buildings; galleries, porches, side-chapels are integrated into their total complex and irregular effect. Above all, tiers of *kokoshniki* (in a typical example such as St Nicholas on the Ordynka, 1647) are by now treated with great delicacy, and become the chief aesthetic element of the building's exterior.

Churches like these point the way forward – particularly through their concern with elegance of outline and their inventively ornamented window surrounds – towards the striking development of Baroque architecture in the last quarter of the seventeenth century. It was extraordinary that Old Russia could gather its strength at so late a stage to produce a final burst of energy that would carry it – without too violent a transition – out of what was still basically a medieval culture into the western-orientated age that followed the Petrine reforms. 'Moscow Baroque' has scarcely received the attention it deserves, whether as a cultural–historical phenomenon or as a period of splendid building activity. Historians have

Moscow, Church of the Intercession in Rubtsovo (1619): cross-section.

Moscow, Church of St Nicholas on the Ordynka (1647).

yet to establish whether at this stage the influx of foreign influences truly predominates over the native tradition, which had so successfully absorbed piecemeal any that had arrived before. The process of joining the European stream of Baroque culture had begun in literature earlier than in architecture; in painting it scarcely took place at all, though developments in the direction of secular portraiture (*parsuny*) have some relevance (see pp. 84–5). An obvious socio-historical condition for it was the mid-seventeenth-century reunification with Muscovy of the Ukraine and West Russian lands – which had experienced, under Polish rule, the normal course of west European cultural development since the Renaissance – and the consequent influx of learned and artistically skilled west Russians (e.g. the poet Simeon of Polotsk) into backward Moscow. This explains some, but not all, aspects of the Moscow Baroque. Ukrainian Baroque architecture had its own features, which are sometimes but not generally to be detected in Great Russia. Moscow Baroque architecture developed, rather, under the direct patronage of a few influential and western-looking noble families (Golitsyns, Naryshkins), who flourished

Fili, near Moscow, Church of the Intercession
(*c.* 1693): south façade.

especially during the minority of Peter the Great. Their churches of the 1680s and 1690s – often on country estates around Moscow (Ubory, Troitse-Lykovo, Fili, Dubrovitsy) – successfully prolong the Old Russian tradition of pyramidality through characteristic diminishing storeys, of varied cross-sections: square, circular, octagonal. At the same time a sumptuously ornate late variant of the old three-bay, more-or-less cubical church is found, particularly in the provinces (Ryazan', Solvychegodsk; note also the main gatehouse church of the Novodevichy Convent, Moscow on p. 61). In many churches (Dubrovitsy; the Ascension in Kadashi, Moscow) splendidly dynamic 'strapwork', curiously reminiscent of Elizabethan England, replaces the older *kokoshniki* in giving particular interest to the roofline. We meet at this period the first architects to stand out as individual personalities: notably Ya. G. Bukhvostov and the two Startsevs. The eve of the Petrine age was in fact a moment of great cultural vitality, within which a varied and original architecture led the way.

Though (as previously in our survey of Old Russian architecture) individual churches form the bulk of material evidence that has come down to us, the Muscovite period for the first time gives us more than isolated examples of other types of building: monastic ensembles, with refectories, cells and bell-towers; defensive walls and towers; public buildings; and

Church at Dubrovitsy, near Podol'sk (1690–1704). Una, Church of St Clement (1501).

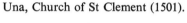

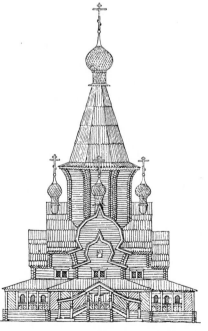

domestic houses. For the first time, too, a fair amount survives from the wooden architecture – mostly but not exclusively ecclesiastical – which was at all times quantitatively dominant in Russia, but no examples of which have been spared from before the Muscovite age (with a single exception: the tiny St Lazarus Church of the Muromsky Monastery on Lake Onega, supposedly built before 1391).

The great monasteries of Russia had always had not only spiritual, but also intellectual, socio-economic and even military significance. During the Muscovite age some of them grew to the dimensions of small cities, with strong encircling walls. Their ensembles are invariably, and no doubt calculatedly, picturesque; their skylines are punctuated with tall bell-towers, whose forms reach an ethereal lightness with such a splendid Moscow Baroque example as that of the Novodevichy Convent. With the strongly centralized governmental organization of the Muscovite age, a certain amount of intentional town-planning could take place. New cities were established in Siberia, while west of Moscow Boris Godunov founded his settlement of Borisov Gorodok, dismantled, alas, in the early nine-teenth century, which was graced by perhaps the most remarkable of Russian tent-churches, 73 metres high; he also completed (1600) the great Moscow Kremlin belfry to a height of no less than 81 metres. In the

Church of St Lazarus from the Muromsky Monastery, now at Kizhi (late fourteenth century): cross-section.

Moscow, Novodevichy Convent: gatehouse church (1680s).

sixteenth century the 'kremlins' of most fortified Russian cities achieved the form in which we see them today: justly famous is that of Smolensk, designed by Fyodor Kon (1596), which required about 100 million bricks; smaller, but also visually impressive, are those of Kolomna and Tula. In Siberia and the north, unlikely as it may seem, fortresses were solidly constructed of wooden logs; towers and fortifications from Bratsk, Yakutsk and elsewhere have survived. During the seventeenth century the dumpy strength of Russian military architecture was made more graceful: fairy-tale towers crowned by lacy strapwork punctuate the walls of the Novodevichy Convent, and the great spires, with their almost Gothic silhouette, are added to the main towers of the Moscow Kremlin (an Englishman, Christopher Galloway, had a hand in their construction). Finally, in 1670–83, an extremely picturesque so-called kremlin was constructed, all of a piece, in the small, ancient town of Rostov: it is really an archbishop's folly, a beguiling pastiche with little functional significance for the age when it was built.

The surviving domestic architecture of Muscovy opens with the curious little late-fifteenth-century palace (much restored) at Uglich, with its plain, four-square plan and good patterned terracotta. Little survives from the sixteenth century, save some monastic refectories; but certain seventeenth-century houses, notably in Pskov, almost certainly preserve the severely plain appearance – with small undecorated windows, large porches and massively vaulted rooms – of an earlier age. In the seventeenth century, however, decorative principles soon extend until the more important domestic buildings are as lively as church architecture (brick- or stone-built houses were still of course an exception: living quarters were often of wood on a stone base, and doubtless better insulated for it). The most notable early surviving example is the residential palace (Teremnoy Dvorets) in the Moscow Kremlin, built by Bazhen Ogurtsov and others in 1635. Thereafter domestic architecture follows an interesting, and until recently insufficiently investigated, course; far more examples

Pskov, the Lapin House (seventeenth century): cross-section.

still stand than used to be thought – well over 100 pre-1700 domestic buildings have been identified in present-day Moscow alone. Particularly impressive are the two or three seventeenth-century 'estates' – ensembles of house, private church and related buildings – that have been partially spared: e.g. that of Averky Kirillov on the Bersenevka, and best of all (since recent restoration) that of the Krutitskoye Podvor'ye, with its covered galleries and its entrance-gate crowned with Osip Startsev's miraculous little *teremok*, completely faced in gorgeously patterned ceramic tiles. Typically, seventeenth-century houses are loosely articulated into unequal sections, with steep-pitched roofs, decorative, often asymmetrically placed pilaster-strips, Dutch gables, outside porches on stumpy, absurd columns, and an inexhaustible variety of decorative window-surrounds, where Old Russian ogees often give place to pseudo-western broken pediments on little engaged columns; such details are usually picked out in white, and the brickwork of the walls is sometimes decorated with a faceted chequerboard pattern or with ceramic tiles.

Wooden architecture – ecclesiastical and domestic – was equally inventive and decorative, and it is sad that much has been destroyed; folk traditions of earlier centuries survived, however, into modern times, and we can guess from later examples at the variety of earlier patterns (the multi-domed churches at Kizhi, the summit of Russian achievement in wood, date from the eighteenth century). Wooden logs – relatively light,

Moscow, Krutitsky Residence (Krutitskoye Podvor'ye), by O. Startsev (late seventeenth century).

strong, carvable and easy to handle – lend themselves to the construction of tall, angular towers and steeply-raked roofs, but not of course to vaults or cylinders; both houses and churches tend to be built in a series of adjacent 'cells' – often, for churches, multi-sided in plan. Large palace-complexes, with a cheerfully uncontrolled variety of forms, could be put together in this way: we are lucky that Catherine II had a model of the huge wooden palace at Kolomenskoye (1667) made before she ordered its demolition. Ordinary houses were – and are – decorated with fretted designs, particularly along the roofline and around the windows.

Yaroslavl', Ipat'yev Monastery, seventeenth-century domestic buildings.

Church of the Transfiguration from Kotlyat'yevo, now at Suzdal' (1754)

Kolomenskoye, wooden palace (1667, now destroyed): reconstruction of south-east façade.

The lusty variegation – even if sometimes leading to vulgarity or triviality – that we have seen in Muscovite architecture was not matched in painting. Nothing to equal the achievements of before 1430 was ever again to be found in Old Russian icons, frescoes or book-illuminations. By about 1500 an 'all-Russian' manner of painting (in which Novgorodian elements were synthesized with Muscovite ones) had obliterated the variety of tendencies and local 'schools' of the preceding age. The last, late master of medieval Russian art was Dionisy, who with his sons painted the beautifully preserved church of the Ferapontov Monastery in 1500; some of the earliest frescoes in the Moscow Dormition Cathedral (1481), and a certain number of icons, can also be attributed to him. His manner has still much of the grace and gentleness of Rublyov, but also a certain bloodlessness, even coldness; it is extremely flat and linear. In general subsequent followers of Rublyov could imitate his obvious trademarks, such as his facial types; but the canons of beauty that lead back from Rublyov to classical antiquity are soon attenuated, and his impressive monumentality – which links him with the oldest traditions of Russian painting, and gives a 'hard edge' even to his tenderest images – proves inimitable. Throughout the sixteenth century large-scale fresco-painting, though it can be pleasant enough, leaves an impression of perfunctoriness and of living on diminishing capital. The same is true of icon-painting which, however, commands rather more interest (if little more aesthetic appeal) through a greater iconographic freedom: complex, multi-figured scenes, often of abstract, sometimes propagandist, significance are produced. Among the more appealing of these are several panels (later fifteenth century) depicting the 'Battle between the Men of Novgorod and the Men of Suzdal", and the remarkable Moscow 'Church Militant' (mid-sixteenth century). Subtlety and dynamism of composition tend to give way to crude symmetry or stiffness; the harmony of glowing colours is forgotten.

The seventeenth century, however, witnessed a modest revival of painting, showing just as did architecture that creative possibilities still lingered within the Old Russian cultural patterns. At the beginning of the century a school of icon-painting, associated particularly with the far north-eastern estates of the Stroganov family, developed a small-scale, bright, doubtless folk-influenced art which had long-lasting effects. With their brilliant intricacy and strong feeling for decorative effect, 'Stroganov' icons are more like small bejewelled objects than paintings. They have an inventiveness and *joie de vivre* which is lacking in even the 'progressive' art of the capital, represented by figures such as I. Vladimirov and the over-praised Simon Ushakov, whose cautious glances westward led to an art of compromise, polished but mostly rather effete. There is more consistency in the aesthetic polemics of their ideological opponent, the

Nazary Istomin, icon of the 'Old Testament Trinity' (1627).

Nikifor Savin, icon of St John the Baptist (early seventeenth century).

Nikita Pavlovets, icon of 'Virgin of the Enclosed Garden' (c. 1670).

archpriest Avvakum, though there is no evidence that the ascetic icon-painting he favoured was on a higher artistic plane than theirs. Some of the most interesting developments in icon-painting of the seventeenth century lead in the direction of realistic portraiture (see pp. 84–5).

Fresco-painting, too, revived most interestingly in the provinces: this time in the city of Yaroslavl', whence a new manner spread to nearby places (Rostov, the Trinity Monastery) and even affected Moscow. Again this is a small-scale, lively art, using bright and harmonious colours, with intricate iconography and – for all its possible folk analogues – considerable sophistication. Western-style perspective effects began to exercise a sporadic influence both on fresco- and icon-painting, and masters of the Yaroslavl' school demonstrably used on occasion western woodcuts (such as those of Piscator's Bible) as general models. Woodcuts, indeed, began to circulate widely in Russia during the seventeenth century, and the same period saw the origin of the *lubok* – the boldly executed illustrative popular print – which was to have a vigorous life in Russia up to the present age. This compensates, perhaps, for the catastrophic decline in manuscript illumination since the fifteenth century; the sketchy illustrations to the great sixteenth-century chronicle compendium, the *Litsevoy svod*, have few artistic pretensions, though they offer a wide-ranging, picturesque and valuable record of Old Russian life.

Lubok (folk woodcut): 'How the Mice buried the Cat', an allegory on the death of Peter I (1730s).

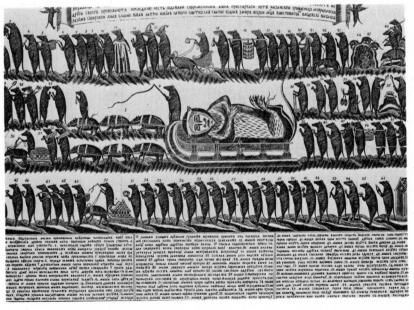

It remains only to make a brief mention of the minor arts of Muscovy. Metalwork of various kinds, enamelling, jewellery, all flourished; from the fifteenth century onwards we have examples of embroidered cloths, usually for liturgical purposes, sometimes designed with a moving directness. In all these forms the Muscovite striving for surface decorativeness at the expense of taste was liable to run riot: the results are often cheerful, usually vulgar. An ostentatious metal casing (*oklad*) is often applied to parts of icons other than faces and hands. More interesting are the developments in wood-carving and ceramics. Many low-relief carved icons have been collected in recent years; sculpture in the round existed

Zagorsk, Trinity Monastery, 'Apparition of Our Lady to Sergius of Radonezh': embroidered altar cloth (sixteenth century).

V. Yermolin, 'St George', painted stone sculpture (late fifteenth century).

Moscow Kremlin, domes of the Church of the 'Saviour behind the Golden Screen', with ceramic decoration (seventeenth century).

too, and part of a forceful St George, set up above the main gate to the Kremlin by V. Yermolin as early as the later fifteenth century, can now be seen in the Tret'yakov Gallery. Sculptures from (usually) provincial churches stand on the borderline between 'high' and 'folk' art, displaying a fine expressiveness. But of all the Muscovite minor arts the development of decorative glazed ceramic tiles was the most characteristic and fruitful. Ceramic exterior decoration of buildings had since Byzantine times been an occasional resource in Orthodox architecture: it assumes far more importance with the great illustrative plaques on the Dmitrov Cathedral (sixteenth, possibly even fifteenth century), gives a final touch of brilliance to churches such as Ostankino and to the eleven picturesque domes of the 'Saviour behind the Golden Screen' in the Kremlin (1680), and reaches its culmination with the casket-like chamber of the Krutitsky Teremok in the very last decade of the seventeenth century.

2

ART AND ARCHITECTURE IN
THE PETERSBURG AGE, 1700-1860

The Petrine reforms had as part of their objective the integration of Russia with the cultural, as well as with the technological achievements of contemporary western Europe. It is common knowledge that in this they succeeded rapidly and overwhelmingly. From the early eighteenth century onwards the art produced in Russia was to be judged by the criteria of European taste, and its history reveals phases, concerns and fashions cognate with, and usually part of, similar phenomena in European art. In general, art henceforth takes the same forms in Russia as elsewhere in the western world, and we apply the same sort of terminology ('Romantic', 'Symbolist', etc.) to Russia's art and indeed to its culture as a whole.

So one is tempted to follow a simple and habitual course among writers on Russia when sketching the history of its art: ruling, so to speak, a neat line through the year 1703 (when St Petersburg was founded) and regarding everything produced on the far side of it as 'Old Russian', qualitatively different from the 'modern European' art which has flourished in Russia since then. Such a view presupposes a complete cultural 'dislocation': 'There had been few moments in the earlier history of art when a change so profound and so sudden occurred as in the reign of Peter the Great in Russia. Moreover, this was a change largely imposed by the ruler himself, and was not an evolution due to the general development of taste, as had occurred in Renaissance Italy.'[1] This presumed dislocation was a cause for pride among, for example, eighteenth- and early nineteenth-century Russians, who felt their nation had belatedly assumed full cultural status; it could be a cause for regret among mid-nineteenth-century (and later) Slavophiles, who felt Russia had sold its individuality, even its soul, to alien and inappropriate influences; it could give pretext for anti-Russian westerners to regard Russia as a barbarian nation perpetually aping cultural achievements which (except with the assistance of foreigners) it could never emulate.

[1] M. Chamot, *Russian Painting and Sculpture* (Oxford, 1963), p. 8.

But the idea of the 'Petrine dislocation' is a half-truth. A change happened, certainly, and its effects were far-reaching; yet it is probably best regarded as one link in a chain of processes that began well before Peter and were completed after his time. It took more than the whim of a powerful sovereign to make the 'westernization' of Russian life feasible. A study of the arts in particular shows a transition that was only super-ficially abrupt, more essentially protracted and complex; real, if concealed, links bind the culture of seventeenth- and early eighteenth-century Russia together. Indeed a modern view of the periodization of Russian cultural history is likely to visualize a distinct period – albeit one of experiment and transition – as stretching from the later seventeenth century down to the 1760s. In art, as to some degree in literature, this can best be char-acterized in western European terms as an 'Age of the Baroque'. Russia's contribution to the European Baroque period was highly individual, varied and worthy of more study and appreciation than it usually attracts. It went through several stages, most clearly marked in architecture – with particularly fruitful climaxes of activity in the last two decades of the seventeenth century and in the reign of Elizabeth (1741–62). Between these, the first four decades of the eighteenth century – mainly the latter part of Peter's reign – actually mark something of a cultural pause, with less of importance going on in the fields of painting or literature, and an architectural reaction towards modesty of scale and sobriety of décor.

The age of 'Classicism' proper[2] succeeds the Baroque in the later eighteenth century (though the term is often loosely used to designate the whole period after the Petrine reforms). With it the westernization of Russian culture can properly be considered as achieved; in an age of conscious internationalism, Russia had acquired full status in the family of nations. Yet reductionists who argue that the arts in Russia are thence-forward 'nothing but' offshoots of their western prototypes ignore several important factors. Works of art are produced and appreciated not in isolation, but within a context: in Russia's case that context embraced the country's history, previous artistic tradition, the system of patronage, religious requirements, notions of what was acceptable, and so on – all adding up to the distinctive 'personality' of Russian art in the period as a whole, even when certain of its individual products may be formally indistinguishable from similar works originating in other countries. Furthermore, Russia achieved its own particular balance between the various arts and the degree of original development they achieved; as previously in Russian history, the most immediately recognizable in-

---

[2] The more specific designations 'Neo-Classicism', 'pseudo-Classicism' (pejorative) and 'Enlightenment Classicism' represent a recognition of the age's status as a definable cultural–historical period; the first of these appears to have become standard western terminology in recent years, while the last is in acceptable usage in Russia.

dividuality was displayed in architecture. Meanwhile Russia's 'folk' and 'vernacular' arts continued to evolve slowly along their own paths, without the sudden stylistic changes characteristic of 'high art' – largely independent of the latter yet not without certain mutual interactions.

Russian Neo-Classicism, like that of western Europe, passed through a series of recognizable stages, ending with a notably attractive version of *style empire* in the early nineteenth century, and fading out into the mid-nineteenth-century eclecticism which in England we should call 'Victorian'. The Romantic movement had comparatively little impact on the visual arts in Russia. In the mid-nineteenth century easel painting takes the place of architecture as the most interesting sphere of Russian art, and before the end of the century is producing masters of international importance – heralding the 'modern movement' of the early twentieth century to which Russia contributed so much. From the mid-nineteenth century, too, the spirit of cultural 'nationalism' (which particularly affected peripheral European countries) turned Russian artists and critics towards a self-conscious examination of the peculiarly Russian aspects of their heritage, inducing them to strengthen or recreate links with the cultural traditions of Old Russia. This movement bore its most immediate fruit in music and perhaps literature; in the visual arts it led eventually to a creative reappraisal of the merits of icon-painting and popular art, which contributed much to the aesthetic of such varied representatives of 'modernism' as Vrubel', Goncharova, Chagall and even Kandinsky. Thus in a sense the 'westernizing episode' in Russian art ended as it began – by the deliberate fusion of a progressive international style with characteristic elements from the native tradition.

The secularization of art

One of the most far-reaching changes that the Baroque age (and Petrine reforms within it) brought to Russia was the secularization of culture. This altered the complexion, or balance, of the arts in Russia as importantly as it did their stylistic developments, and indeed it determined many of the latter. Thus in the early eighteenth century icon-painting – for 700 years one of the leading areas of achievement in Russian culture – drops out of the territory of 'high art' altogether. It was not simply a question of a decline in quality (such declines had happened earlier); nor, paradoxically, was this change of status marked by important stylistic changes. Indeed, the crux of the matter is that the steady process of stylistic development and variegation which had been characteristic of icon-painting up to the later seventeenth century now came to an end. Icons thus became what to the vulgar western imagination they have generally seemed – a 'stereotyped' art-form. The products of this art can

73

have plenty of charm, springing from reminiscences of its greater days; but flexibility, grandeur, liveliness and evolutionary potential are all lost. In fact, so far as any variegation does enter into post-Baroque icon-painting, its effect is yet more disastrous: elements of debased western religious painting are often awkwardly grafted on to the static Russian stereotypes to produce sentimental *bondieuseries*. It is indicative that the *oklad* (decorative metal casing) of an icon becomes more and more important, often resulting in the near-concealment of the painted surface itself.

However, the loss of 'high art' status did not prejudice the exploitation of icon-painting as a folk art, in parts of the country sufficiently isolated from mechanistic icon-production to escape its baneful effect. Here the popular traditions of Russian religious art continued through the seventeenth and eighteenth centuries, and well into the nineteenth, without dislocation or serious degeneration. Certain villages – notably Palekh and Mstyora – developed local traditions of craftsmanship in the painting of intricate, small-figured, brightly-coloured icons; nowadays these villages produce similarly executed scenes from folk tales on papier-mâché boxes and trays, with a formalized delicacy which puts them among the most unusual and sought-after forms of Russian folk-art.

Wall-painting in churches – so dynamic and rich through the whole history of pre-Petrine Russia, capable of evolving new and satisfying modes of expression right up to the late seventeenth century – largely shares the fate of icon-painting, an art form closely related to it. The introduction of western post-Renaissance pictorial elements is here if anything more widespread, though the results are not quite as uniformly disastrous: after all, leading secular painters from Antropov to Vrubel' produced work (though seldom their best) in this field. Yet religious mural painting after Peter was as a whole even less interesting than icon-painting, since it lacked the latter's saving possibilities of development on a folk-art level.

Religious sculpture, however, occupies a position of its own in the seventeenth and eighteenth centuries. Though Old Russian (and Byzantine) sculpture is an under-investigated subject, enough evidence survives to let us conclude that – contrary to what was until recently supposed – sculpture, chiefly in wood, was a flourishing form of art throughout the Old Russian period. But it seldom seems to have achieved the full acceptance from church and state authorities that would have enabled it to develop on the plane of 'high art'. It remained one of the most striking expressions of the folk traditions of Russian art, and as such it continued to flourish into the eighteenth century. In the 1720s the Synod of the Church pronounced against religious sculpture, and it can be assumed that much was destroyed then. But in peripheral regions, notably Perm' and Vologda, the traditional carved and painted wood figures continued to be produced

74

despite this ordinance, and in their monumental expressiveness constitute one of the noblest, if least known, forms of later Russian vernacular art. This tradition has no direct connexion, of course, with the secular sculpture of the eighteenth century – the most 'western' of the art forms introduced by Peter, and primarily in the hands of foreigners until the latter part of the century – unless it be through the person of the important sculptor Fyodor Shubin, who grew up among the peasant wood-carvers of the north.

Architecture was less radically affected by the 'secularization' of culture than were the other arts. Churches and cathedrals continued to form a major part of Russian architecture throughout the eighteenth and early nineteenth centuries, and in them the ecclesiastical architecture of the previous age was evolved and adapted to new taste, rather than super-seded: after a flirtation with basilican ground-plans under Peter, variants of the centralized 'cross-in-square' soon reassert their primacy. Nevertheless secular monuments were quantitatively, and often qualitatively, domi-

'Christ in Captivity', sculpture in painted wood (eighteenth century, Vologda).

St Petersburg, Cathedral of SS Peter and Paul (D. Trezzini, 1712): ground-plan.

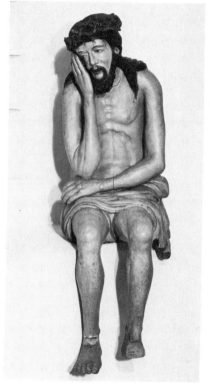

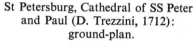

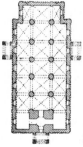

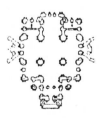

St Petersburg, Cathedral of Smol′ny Convent (V. V. Rastrelli 1746): ground-plan.

nant, and secular decorative principles held sway. There are few great monastic ensembles to stand comparison with those of the sixteenth and seventeenth centuries. But the tall, stepped bell-towers of the eighteenth century directly continue pre-Petrine traditions.

Petersburg Baroque (1700s–1760s)

During the 'Petersburg Baroque' age (i.e. until the 1760s) architecture retained the pre-eminence among the arts of Russia which it had held for the previous couple of centuries. Not only had this been prepared for by the unprecedented architectural activity of the 1690s: from 1703 (the establishment of St Petersburg) opportunities on the grandest scale opened before it. For the first time the need for the coherent planning of a city opens before Russian architects. Not that Peter relied for this primarily on his compatriots: early schemes were drawn up by foreigners such as the famous German Schlüter, the Italian-Swiss Trezzini (Trezini in Russian) and the Frenchman Leblond. From the latter's plans, however, only the grid of streets on Vasil'yev Island has had lasting importance. The shape of the city developed its own dynamism, and eventually settled down about the axial line of the Nevsky Prospekt, intersected by a series of canals and broad ring roads – something doubtless unforeseen and unintended in the early eighteenth century.

This is perhaps the place for a note, even if very brief, on the foreign artists encouraged to settle in Russia during the eighteenth century. It is impossible to write a history of Russian art without them, and equally it is impossible to include them all in a history of Russian art. Figures as considerable as the painter Louis Caravaque and the architect Rinaldi, important as they seemed in their day, are ultimately peripheral. Others (notably the architects Trezzini, Quarenghi and Cameron) made contributions of the greatest value to Russian culture, and did so by working in its spirit and developing its potentialities. The greatest of them all – V. V. Rastrelli – was a foreigner only in name, more correctly a second-generation Russian: for he settled in the country as a boy with his sculptor father, and both lived there the rest of their days. Rossi, Fel'ten (Velten), Bove were among several architects Russian-born of immigrant families.

Architecture
The transition from Old Russian to modern architecture makes a fascinating study; Russian architecture around 1700 was teeming with ideas and innovations. It would appear that the earliest buildings (apart from those in the 'Foreign Suburb' of Moscow) showing awareness of western principles of proportion, symmetry and the classic use of orders slightly antedate the foundation of Petersburg; they probably included

the first palace at Lefortovo (Moscow), started by D. Aksamitov in 1697, the church at Marfino (1701) and the severe Arsenal building – subsequently much altered – in the Moscow Kremlin (K. Konrad and D. Ivanov, 1702), which, with its rusticated lower storey and paired windows, turns out to have been eccentric to the main path of subsequent Russian architecture. What, though, are we to make of the earlier tower-church at Dubrovitsy (1690) in which a mass of innovatory western detail, and a novel centralized ground-plan, fail to eradicate our impression of an Old Russian (rather than classical European) building? Or of the two great Moscow churches by I. P. Zarudny, the 'Men'shikov Tower' (1705) and St John the Warrior (1709), where old and new decorative and

Moscow, 'Men'shikov Tower', Church of the Archangel Gabriel (I. P. Zarudny, 1705).

structural features are perhaps more delicately balanced than anywhere else? Or of the series of buildings, several of them inspired if not designed by Peter himself, which feature stepped multi-storey towers: the now demolished Pharmacy on Red Square and the Sukharev Tower (1692), the Utich′ya Tower at Zagorsk (late seventeenth century), SS Peter and Paul on the New Basmannaya, Moscow (1705), Mattarnovi's Kunstkamera in Petersburg (1718) – or stepped tower with spire: the Men′shikov Tower, the old Admiralty in Petersburg (1704, remodelled 1732), Trezzini's cathedral in the Peter–Paul Fortress (1712)? Some of these buildings seem formally Old Russian, others westernized, yet the links between them are so clear that we have reason to speak of a 'transitional style', full of variety and invention, sometimes clumsy, always vigorous. If one building sums up what the new Russia of this period owed to the old, it might be the Kunstkamera: ostensibly classical in all details, yet with the semi-disciplined cheerfulness of Muscovy about the articulation of its

St Petersburg, Kunstkamera (J. Mattarnovi *et al.*, 1718): reconstruction of façade.

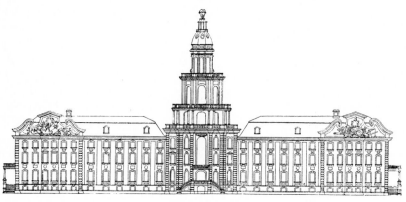

St Petersburg, Fortress and Cathedral of SS Peter and Paul (D. Trezzini, 1712), viewed across the River Neva.

façade, the broad decorativeness of its white pseudo-pilaster strips, its pitched roofs, the unexpected octagon of its tower. It makes a splendid foil to the huge Admiralty across the River Neva.

The primary building material of the new city's main structures (as is true for most periods and places in the history of Russian architecture) was brick. 'White stone' (limestone), in eighteenth-century Petersburg and Moscow, was employed if at all in half-basement storeys, columns and other details of the façade. But whereas in later Muscovite architecture the brickwork was left exposed, to be treated in a highly decorative manner with 'white stone', carved and coloured brick or ceramic details, in the architecture of 'Europeanized' Russia the same impulse towards polychrome decorativeness of the façade is achieved quite differently. The walls are completely stuccoed and colour-washed in plain tints – most often yellow, sometimes green, red, orange, blue, pink or purple. Details such as cornices and pilasters are picked out in white, and the *nalichnik* (ornamental window frame) continues to have as important a decorative function during the Petersburg Baroque age as it had in the seventeenth century. Sometimes this treatment is applied to colonnades, and even

St Petersburg, 'model houses' designed by Trezzini (1714): (*top*) for humble, (*middle*) for well-to-do and (*bottom*) for wealthy inhabitants.

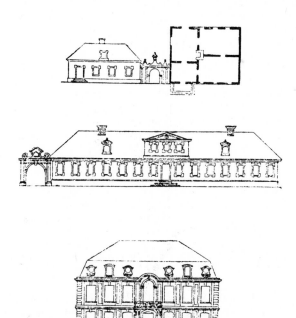

whole buildings, constructed in wood rather than brick. The unforced gaiety of colour-washed façades adds one of the most characteristic (and, to the visitor, least expected) notes to the visual charm of Russian architecture.

Despite the vigour of the 'transitional' style, a certain note of sobriety informs the architecture of Peter's Russia, particularly in the later years of his reign. This is naturally well seen in the unpretentious 'model houses' devised (1714) by Trezzini for the humble, middling and wealthy inhabitants of the new city (a number of domestic buildings in similar taste are also to be found in Moscow). But this sobriety shows too in buildings with grander purposes: Peter's Summer Palace (1708), the original parts of Peterhof, the Men'shikov Palace (1710), the Peter-Paul fortress itself. More imposingly Baroque, though still restrained, were the palaces at Strel'na (1725) and Oranienbaum (1710), Zemtsov's Hall of Ceremonies (1725) near the Summer Palace, and Trezzini's most daring contribution to the Petersburg townscape: the 'Twelve Colleges' (i.e. Ministries, 1721), now housing Leningrad University, which were strung end-to-end across the tip of Vasil'yev Island.

Peter's famous decree of 1714 had forbidden stone or brick building in Moscow and other cities so as to concentrate resources in his new capital. Its significance can easily be exaggerated, however; it was soon relaxed, and at no stage entirely effective. The exquisite church of the Zaikonospassky Monastery seems to date largely from that time, as does the oldest

Peterhof, The Great Palace (1714, enlarged by Rastrelli 1745) and park (sculpture by Kozlovsky *et al.*); from an early nineteenth-century watercolour.

surviving country house near Moscow, Glinki. But the later 1720s and the 1730s, after Peter's death, were nowhere a period of bold activity or innovation in Russian architecture. They were rather years of consolidation: M. G. Zemtsov (1688–1743) and the Petersburg 'Building Commission' began to mould the young city in its modern shape; I. A. Mordvinov and the best Russian-born architect of the age, I. F. Michurin (1700–63), put the planning of Moscow on a more ordered footing; P. M. Yeropkin (d. 1740) prepared an important architectural treatise; I. Korobov and Michurin were influential teachers, from whose tutelage emerged two of the key figures of the next, 'Elizabethan', stage of the Baroque: Chevakinsky and Ukhtomsky.

The achievements of these two decades, the 1740s and 1750s, almost coinciding with the reign of the Empress Elizabeth, have a grandeur unparalleled in the history of Russian architecture. They make a fitting climax to the entire Baroque age; they represent the most remarkable synthesis of what Europe could contribute to Russia and Russia to Europe in the first century of westernization. It is as if all the exuberance and colourfulness of Old Russia were reincarnated in the swelling forms, broken pediments, massed engaged columns, sculptural window-surrounds, polychrome decoration and gilded domes of Smol'ny, of Tsarskoye Selo, of the 'Marine' Cathedral and of the Winter Palace.

The period is associated above all with the name of V. V. Rastrelli (1700–76). His earliest independent work apparently dates from the beginning of the 1720s; his first masterpiece from 1741–4, when he made the designs (realized subsequently by Michurin) for St Andrew's Church in Kiev. In 1745 he enlarged Peterhof, and in 1746 began to create his huge and magnificent project for the Smol'ny Convent in Petersburg for the Empress. This had a complicated subsequent history, and what would have been the greatest monastic ensemble of the post-Petrine age was never fully realized; luckily Rastrelli's model survives, and enables us to admire

St Petersburg, the 'Twelve Colleges' by Trezzini (1721): fragment of façade.

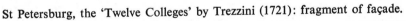
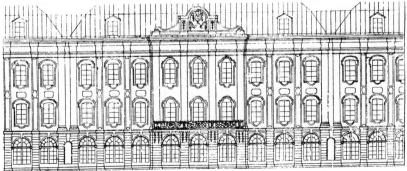

the daring of the great, slim belfry that was never built. In the early 1750s his activity was astonishing: the Vorontsov and Stroganov Palaces, the remodelling of the Great Palace at Tsarskoye Selo (incorporating the blocks designed in similar, if less luxuriant, taste by Kvasov and Chevakinsky in the 1740s), and finally the Winter Palace, last of a succession occupying the site, which was begun in 1754. Huge as this building is, it

St Petersburg, Bridge of Nevsky Prospekt over the River Moyka; corner of Stroganov Palace (Rastrelli, 1753).

St Petersburg, Winter Palace (Rastrelli, 1754). *Foreground:* Alexander Column (Montferrand, 1834).

is in no way oppressive; its grandeur is a domestic grandeur, relieved by the cheerfulness of its roofline statuary and ornament, its colour-washed walls and the subtle rhythm of its white columns. It is perfectly integrated with its urban setting, and its immensely long, rambling façade neither dominates nor is rendered insignificant by the magnificent expanse of the broad river in front of it – forming a view comparable only to that across the Giudecca Canal in Venice. The Winter Palace's modest three storeys set a ceiling on subsequent building which has helped to preserve the marvellous visual wholeness of Petersburg/Leningrad to this day.

The other architects of Rastrelli's age are by no means merely his imitators. They may sometimes seem a little staid in comparison with his exuberance; but all of them made individual and memorable contributions to the spirit of Elizabethan Baroque. Chevakinsky's masterpiece is the St Nicholas 'Marine' Cathedral (1752) in Petersburg, Kvasov's the cathedral at Kozelets (1748). In Moscow the presiding figure, his influence rivalling Rastrelli's in Petersburg, was D. V. Ukhtomsky (1719–75), who with Michurin was responsible for the great bell-tower of the Trinity–Sergius Monastery (now Zagorsk). St Clement's Church in Moscow (begun in the 1740s) is the most prominent 'Elizabethan' building in the city; its stately five-domed outline shows the revivification in the mid-eighteenth century of traditional Russo–Byzantine concepts of church architecture. A single fine domestic building, the Apraksin house on the Pokrovka (Chernyshevsky Street) – probably the last significant Russian Baroque structure (1766), by an unknown architect – survives to demonstrate that the dynamic Baroque typical of Rastrelli had a foothold in the older capital. With one or two late examples in provincial cities the style is brought to a close.

Moscow, Apraksin House (1766).

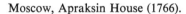

Painting

Dominant as architecture is in Russia until the 1760s, we should not let it totally overshadow the more modest, yet still important development of easel painting. Peter the Great approved of painting (for practical rather than purely aesthetic reasons) and sent several young artists to western Europe for training. West European painters in turn came to Russia; and the aesthetic principles of western art and its techniques (e.g. oil painting) were adopted in Russia as quickly as other western civilizational norms. However, though the main genres established themselves early, one alone predominated throughout the eighteenth century and beyond: portraiture.

This demonstrates the significant concealed links which make the transition from the Old Russian to the modern period less of a dislocation in painting (as in architecture) than might have been expected. For by the start of the eighteenth century portraiture had already – within the aesthetic framework of Old Russian art – risen to quite significant status and quality. The representation of living personages was perfectly normal in Byzantine, and subsequently Russian mural painting. Donor portraits are, indeed, common in medieval churches, and though these are often hieratic and formalized, many show an evident attempt to fix the individual features of the subject. From the early seventeenth century portraiture, no longer only on walls, but on panels – basically using the techniques of icon-painting – becomes a recognizable art-form. A well-known early example is the remarkable 'icon' of Prince Skopin-Shuysky (1587–1610) which was hung over his tomb; other eminent personages were similarly honoured. Thus developed the curious, perhaps under-investigated genre

Parsuna (portrait icon) of Tsar Fyodor (seventeenth century).

I. Vishnyakov, 'Sarah Fermor' (1750s).

of the *parsuna* (a word derived through Polish from the Latin *persona*) which became more and more important as the seventeenth century proceeded, and which continued to have an effect even on 'westernized' portraiture until the second half of the eighteenth century. Renewed links with the west Russian and Ukrainian lands (which were already familiar with post-Renaissance art through Poland) strengthened this tendency, and visiting foreigners even painted some purely western-style portraits – notably that of the Patriarch Nikon and his associates (now in the Historical Museum, Moscow). In general *parsuny* primarily aim to fix and commemorate the features of great men, as their derivation from icon-painting would lead one to expect. It was in the same spirit, no doubt, that Peter encouraged portraits and busts of himself. But already before his programme of westernization was fully under way he had adapted and parodied the *parsuna* genre in a series of portraits of his 'Unholy Synod' (the best known is that of Yakov Turgenev, 1698).

The transition to western post-Renaissance methods in painting thus involved no crisis for Russian art. 'Picture-space' and perspective – Renaissance developments *par excellence* – are by their nature less likely to be of primary importance in close-up portraiture than in other forms of painting. While the main Russian portraitists of the first half and middle of the eighteenth century – A. Antropov (1716–95), I. Argunov (1727–1802), A. Matveyev (1701–39), I. Vishnyakov (1699–1761) – were neither naïve nor lacking in western skills, features pointing back to the *parsuna* emerge in many of their most characteristic, indeed attractive works: reliance on draughtsmanship rather than modelling or picture-space, lack of interest in facial expression, concern with surface decorativeness. The considerable similarities here to the art of European countries where Renaissance lessons were only gradually assimilated (as in sixteenth- and seventeenth-century England) are no accident. Probably the most attractive work in this manner is Vishnyakov's 'Sarah Fermor' (1750s); Antropov's famous portrait of the Cossack *Ataman* Krasnoshchokov (1761) is a late and striking example of it. All the more remarkable in this context is the work of Ivan Nikitin (d. 1741), showing little or no trace of *parsuna* influences (which are even to be found in portraits by his brother Roman). I. Nikitin is probably best remembered for a masterly and expressive portrait of Peter the Great (Russian Museum, Leningrad).

Sculpture
Peter adorned the formal gardens of his new residences with appropriate statuary; free-standing, western-style sculpture in fact appeared as early as the church at Dubrovitsy (1690–1704) and on Peter's new bridge at Voronezh (1699), and it later formed an integral part of the décor of the Winter Palace. At this period, however, true sculpture had not yet properly

integrated itself into the native Russian cultural scheme – though intricate carving and moulding were of prime importance in the decoration of buildings throughout the history of old Russian architecture, and wooden sculpture (see above) flourished as a folk tradition. Elaborately carved and gilded wooden iconostases are a characteristic art-form of the seventeenth to eighteenth centuries. By far the most important sculptor of the Russian Baroque was C.-B. Rastrelli (1675–1744), father of the architect, who came to Petersburg in 1716. He designed a striking, formal equestrian statue of Peter, which now stands at the approaches to the 'Engineers' Castle', Leningrad, and made well-known portrait busts of the monarch.

The minor and applied arts of Russia need at this stage only a brief mention: until the 1760s they are comparatively little developed, and the decorative traditions of Old Russia have not been seriously challenged. But the experiments of the polymath M. Lomonosov (1711–65) – better known in his roles as Russia's greatest Baroque poet and first important scientist – at reviving the art of mosaic were not without interest. A fine series of mid-eighteenth-century pictorial tapestries, showing vigorous and fantastic scenes, hang in Peter's Mon Plaisir residence at Peterhof; a State tapestry workshop had been set up (with French weavers) in 1717.

C.-B. Rastrelli, monument to Peter I, with part of 'Engineers' Castle' (Palace of St Michael, V. I. Bazhenov).

C.-B. Rastrelli, 'Peter I', in bronze (1723).

The age of Neo-Classicism (1760s – mid-nineteenth century)

Russian Baroque art scarcely, if at all, passed through a Rococo phase. There is a solidity even about Rastrelli (perhaps thrust upon him by the nature of his commissions) which places him, rather, in the full-blooded Baroque tradition. Painting, because of the unusual circumstances of its development (as outlined above), was the least overtly 'Baroque' of the arts in any case. We might look for Rococo features, if anywhere, in the minor arts of furniture and interior décor; perhaps also in a few paintings such as the portrait of Peter III by Antropov (1762), in certain youthful works of Rokotov and Levitsky, and in such architectural schemes as the un-realized house-plans of F. Argunov (1716–*c*.1768). But in fact Russian Baroque, having come to the edge of the Rococo, suddenly turned away – taking the path which led in a quite different direction, towards 'Neo-' (or 'Enlightenment') Classicism.

This change of direction was, of course, part of a general European movement which (inspired by such thinkers as Diderot, Winckelmann, Lessing, Rousseau) set up simplicity and naturalness as ideals in opposition to Baroque intricacy and theatricality, sought a truer understanding of classical Roman and (particularly) Greek values, and fostered the in-dividual sensibility in which early Romanticism was to be deeply rooted. In Russia its effects pervaded all areas of cultural life, and were astonish-ingly productive and long-lived. When Romanticism came to Russia, its values scarcely clashed with those of the Enlightenment, of which indeed Russian Romanticism looked more or less like an offshoot (the position of Pushkin in literature is particularly indicative of this). It marks the period when, from the European viewpoint, Russia culturally 'came of age'; with native-born Russians contributing at a level of high sophistica-tion not merely to the architecture and portrait-painting which had always been well developed in Russia, but to sculpture, to landscape and other pictorial genres, to porcelain, to all forms of minor and applied art – and, on the wider cultural front, to literature, music, aesthetic and social thought, and educational theory. The age's conscious spirit of 'inter-nationalism' tended to erase, but never obliterated, Russia's cultural idiosyncrasies, while assisting the fruitful circulation of ideas and tech-niques. Artistic education and organization were put on a more ordered footing (the Academy of Arts was founded in 1757), while an art collection of international importance was built up at the Hermitage in Petersburg. Just as the last phase of Russian Baroque was associated with the reign of Elizabeth, so was Enlightenment Classicism with that of Catherine the Great – though its first manifestations precede her, it long outlived her, and the contribution of her personal taste and intellect to the culture of the Russian Enlightenment was somewhat equivocal and ultimately dis-appointing.

In architecture, painting and sculpture the first Neo-Classicist generation – artists who came to maturity in the early 1760s – not only stand out as some of the greatest that the period produced, but occupy a somewhat special position within it as compared with their successors. Their work retains certain memories of the preceding age, and a hint of the luxuriance and theatricality of the full-blooded Baroque, of the delicacy and playfulness of incipient Rococo, still warms and invigorates them. There was no danger of their being infected by the potential aridity and pettiness which could threaten later, 'Empire', Classicism. Of this generation the greatest names in architecture are Bazhenov and Kazakov, in painting Levitsky and Rokotov (also the less gifted, though historically important Losenko), in sculpture Shubin. A more-or-less comparable figure in literature would be the fine poet G. R. Derzhavin (b. 1743), who is similarly able to synthesize elements that look back to the Baroque, and even forward to early Romanticism, with his basic Neo-Classicism. However, there is no such clearcut division (temporally or stylistically) between this and the succeeding generations as there was, for example, at the end of the Baroque period, and so we shall examine the various main branches of art over the Neo-Classical period as a whole, despite any temptation to treat the generation of the 1730s as a separate, 'transitional' period.

Architecture

From the 1760s to the 1840s architectural activity becomes so widespread in Russia, and the surviving buildings are so numerous, that it is impossible in an outline such as this even to list (let alone to discuss) anything but certain outstanding architects and their works. This is the period when the main cities of Russia take the shape with which we are familiar to this day; new ones are founded (including Odessa) and many old towns to a greater or lesser extent replanned (e.g. Poltava, Kostroma, Tver'). The great country houses – met with throughout Russia, but particularly characteristic of the hinterland of the two capitals – nearly all date in their ultimate development from this time. Though much work is done in Petersburg, so that the great Nevsky Prospekt (for example) takes on the basic appearance by which we know it now, the city loses its earlier architectural hegemony. It would not be perverse to say that Moscow's contribution to the architecture of Enlightenment Classicism is more outstanding, and somehow more characteristic than that of Petersburg. In any case it was with Moscow that the first great native architects of the new style are primarily associated.

In Russian – especially Petersburg – architecture the transition to Neo-Classicism is startlingly abrupt. It seems to have originated in an 'anti-Baroque reaction'; Rastrelli's dominance was overthrown when in 1761 (still in the reign of Elizabeth) his plans for the Gostinyy Dvor (market halls) were rejected, and the commission given to a young French architect, J.-B. Vallin de la Mothe. Other key buildings in the new manner also date from 1761; evidently the transition had nothing to do with the tastes of Catherine II (who came to the throne in 1762) as commentators have mostly assumed. Appropriately, the new Academy of Arts was one of the early grandiose Neo-Classic products (1765): a cold, rather un-Russian masterpiece by Vallin de la Mothe and A. F. Kokorinov. The former also designed the Hermitage (1764), which contrasts interestingly with the adjoining Winter Palace. A lighter touch, and more evident memories of the preceding age, characterize the work of A. Rinaldi (c. 1710–94), who rebuilt the palace of Oranienbaum; his Katal′naya Gorka (Toboggan Hill, 1760), in its grounds, is almost a little Baroque *jeu*. His most famous building is the Petersburg 'Marble Palace' (1768), untypically faced with marble and granite rather than stuccoed.

In Moscow, however, the first great architects of Enlightenment Classicism were native-born Russians. In their education an important role was played by D. V. Ukhtomsky; it is worth noting that his variant of the Baroque style is altogether more sober and 'classical' than that of Rastrelli, and the leap forward to Bazhenov's 'neo-mannerist' concepts is not a huge one. But first we must mention the slightly older K. I. Blank (1728–93): very popular in his time, he is somewhat neglected now, but was an important 'transitional' figure. He helped Rastrelli to restore the monastery of New Jerusalem, with its magnificent Baroque rotunda (destroyed in the last war); he is best known for the huge Foundling Hospital (1764) on the Moscow River just below the Kremlin, startlingly severe for its date, almost barrack-like – a reflection of its function. With its heavy cornice, poverty of decoration and unengaging tower, this

Kuskovo, near Moscow, 'Hermitage' (K. I. Blank, mid-eighteenth century).

building has no intention of charming. It is a world away from Blank's masterpiece, the elegant little Moscow church known as 'Nikola v Zvonaryakh' (1760), which still has considerable sense of the Baroque about its dome, and from his series of delightful buildings in the park of Kuskovo. Petersburg had its equivalent transitional architect in the person of Yu. M. Fel'ten (1730–1801), designer of the cheerful Armenian Church on Nevsky Prospekt.

V. I. Bazhenov (1737–99) can claim to be regarded as one of the greatest, or at least most inventive, European architects of his time. Yet not only is he nowadays little regarded abroad–in his lifetime he was unable to take advantage of opportunities fitting for his genius, and only a handful of buildings by him have survived (even among these the attribution is not in all cases clearly established). His gifts were early recognized, though he was of humble birth; after early contact with Ukhtomsky in Moscow and Chevakinsky in Petersburg, followed by study at the newly established Academy of Arts, he travelled and studied with brilliant success in France and Italy during the early 1760s. As early as 1767 he embarked on his grandest project: at the behest of Catherine II he drew up plans for an entire new palace complex, integrated with the ancient buildings, within the Moscow Kremlin. In the mid-1770s the money ran out, and Bazhenov's scheme never rose above its complex foundations – though it became famous through his plans and model. Judging by these, one can hazard the opinion that the façade overlooking the Moscow River, with its great upper-storey colonnade, would have been of a sober magnificence comparable only with Diocletian's Palace at Split.

Tsaritsyno, near Moscow, 'Gothic' buildings by V. I. Bazhenov (1775): reconstruction.

Bazhenov's second great uncompleted project, also for Catherine, was begun soon after the abandonment of the Kremlin palace, and was to waste a full decade of his life. This was for an entire architectural ensemble, consisting of palace, outbuildings and various follies, at Tsaritsyno near Moscow. These were commissioned and executed in the neo-Gothic manner – an early example of this for anywhere in Europe, let alone for Russia, which of course had no indigenous Gothic tradition. Bazhenov may in fact have experimented with Gothic forms even earlier, in, e.g., the church at Cherkizovo near Kolomna. At Tsaritsyno he does so with typical eighteenth-century tastefulness, and with a superb sense of landscape-planning. However, Catherine became displeased with Bazhenov and his plans: she ordered the nearly completed palace to be razed, and handed over the work to Kazakov (who completed it in his own mode of neo-Gothic).

Bazhenov's greatest standing work is the Pashkov House (subsequently the Rumyantsev, now part of the Lenin Library) in Moscow, begun in 1784. Again his gift for perfect siting comes into play: the house, with its pavilions and outbuildings, crowns a slope looking across to the Kremlin walls and the Moscow River. Its tall proportions, the richness of its fluted composite columns and pilasters, its balustrades at ground and roof level, its elegant small dome have all been used to create a gravely impressive but in no way ponderous architectural effect. Bazhenov soon afterwards designed another important domestic building in Moscow – the Yushkov House (21 Kirov Street) – in a style closer to that of 'standard' (neo-Palladian) Russian Classicism, but making dramatic use of a jutting,

Moscow, Pashkov House (attributed to V. I. Bazhenov, 1784).

rounded corner. In Petersburg his last and best-known work is the curious palace now known as the 'Engineers' Castle', begun for the neurotic Tsar Paul in 1797, and completed – with detrimental changes – after Bazhenov's death by his assistant Brenna. In this strange commission (a moated castle translated into eighteenth-century terms!) Bazhenov's bleakly opulent mannerism comes fully into its own.

Matvey Kazakov (1738–1813) had all the luck which his contemporary and colleague Bazhenov missed. Setting his sights rather lower, he was able to realize many more commissions in the course of his long career. He is the architect of Moscow Classicism *par excellence*, neither studying abroad nor working in Petersburg. Typically his buildings are large country or town houses, plainer in style than Bazhenov's grander projects; a touch of the latter's dynamic inventiveness is felt, however, in such (centrally-planned) buildings as Petrovskoye-Alabino, the mausoleum at Nikol'skoye-Pogoreloye, the Church of St Philip the Metropolitan. In public

Moscow, Senate building in the Kremlin by M. F. Kazakov (1776).

commissions he is capable of great dignity and severity: he was Blank's assistant in designing the Foundling Hospital (see pp. 89–90), and built the clean-cut, unobtrusive Senate in the Kremlin (1776). The first Moscow University (1786) was rather less austere, his larger private houses (notably those of the Razumovsky, Demidov and Gubin families) and the Golitsyn Hospital (1796) much less so. Much play is made with perky, flattened, sometimes oddly fenestrated domes. Perhaps his taste was less sure than some of his contemporaries': his chief excursion into antiquarianism, the Petrovsky Palace (1775), is an ugly building, in which an excess of spiky Gothic and stumpy Old Russian detail is applied to a solidly plain domed house. Something more like Bazhenov's wit and taste inform Kazakov's Gothic rebuilding of Tsaritsyno (1786; see above). But his contribution to Russian architecture is thoroughly individual and at its best unsurpassed; some of his finest work, incidentally, is to be found in his interiors – of which the most famous is the 'Hall of Columns', in the present-day Dom Soyuzov.

A host of admirable architects born in the decade or so after Bazhenov and Kazakov show less of their individuality, fewer quirks and a purer approach to Classical principles. They include such figures as N. A. L'vov, Ye. T. Sokolov (the Petersburg Public Library, 1795), Rodion Kazakov (presumed designer of the Batashov house in Moscow), F. Camporesi (whose designs for the magnificent wooden theatre-palace of Ostankino were reworked by a team of serf architects, 1792), and two architects of genius: I. Ye. Starov (1744–1808) and G. Quarenghi (1744–1817), an enthusiast for Palladio who settled in Russia from 1779. Of comparable brilliance, but standing a little apart, is the Scots-born Charles Cameron (1746–1812).

Starov's grandest assignments were the cathedral of the Alexander Nevsky Monastery in Petersburg (1778) and the palace at nearby Pella. The latter was soon demolished; the former is too ponderous to be altogether satisfying or typical, integrating awkwardly with the cheerful range of monastic buildings dating back to Trezzini. So Starov's name lives primarily for the Tauride Palace (1783), large in scale yet (with its long, single-storey galleries) in no way overwhelming. His smaller country houses show dashing originality: Taitsy near Petersburg (1774), and

Moscow, Gubin House by M. F. Kazakov (1780s).

93

particularly Nikol'skoye-Gagarino near Moscow (1773), whose bold curves have an almost Baroque dynamism. He was a notable figure in the town-planning and reconstruction characteristic of the later eighteenth century. Quarenghi's buildings are among the most assuredly tasteful to emerge from the whole period of Russian Classicism, whose spirit he perfectly absorbed while bringing to it a geometrically severe interpretation of Palladianism. Two of them – the Hermitage Theatre (1782) in Petersburg and the Alexander Palace (1792) at Tsarskoye Selo – stand close to Rastrelli's masterpieces, with which they make a remarkably cool contrast. The most prominent is the dazzling, stark Academy of Sciences (1783) on the Neva waterfront near the Kunstkamera.

Cameron too came to Russia (to work for Catherine) in 1779. A Jacobite, he had spent much time in France and Italy; he had studied at first hand the forms of Roman architecture and decoration, which he reproduced with the carefully observed delicacy characteristic of the English Adam style. The marvellous covered gallery (1783) which he designed for Catherine's promenades at Tsarskoye seems to float upon air. He was a master of the

Tsarskoye Selo (Pushkin), 'Cameron Gallery' of the Great Palace (1783).

Pavlovsk, near St Petersburg, the palace (1782): reconstruction of original plan of façade by C. Cameron.

'total' work of architecture, paying as much attention to interior decoration as to external form and setting in landscape: and the Russian landscape, with its delicately varied note of understatement, seems perfectly tailored to his vision. He seems to have built little, but in Pavlovsk (1782 onwards), with its modest domed palace, pavilions, rivers, lakes and groves, he and his assistants produced an ensemble which seems to sum up all that Russian country-house architecture was striving towards.

The high achievements of the 1770s and 80s were never quite to be emulated afterwards. Yet Russian Classical architecture of the early nineteenth century has plenty to its credit. If a certain coldness and repetitiousness sometimes begin to be felt, if in the largest public buildings there is an uneasy striving for effect, nevertheless there is also a high general level of taste, a delicacy of detail and proportion inherited and developed from Starov, Quarenghi and Cameron. With one important exception, it is in the middling and lesser buildings of the period that these widespread virtues are most manifest. In the eighteenth century the great Moscow town houses had often had the spaciousness more normal on country estates, with main façades set well back within projecting side wings; now they are usually more modest in size, standing flush with the pavement, and together can form as notable a piece of townscape as the Prechistenka (now Kropotkin Street). For Moscow, of course, this period has special significance, since the fire of 1812 led to vast rebuilding activity in the years immediately following. But it affected Petersburg too, even if it had less of a formative role in the making of the city as we now see it; it was there that the two finest Russian buildings of the age were erected (the new Admiralty and the Stock Exchange) as well as two of the most prominent (the Kazan' and St Isaac's Cathedrals). Several new architects made their names in this later period: among the more memorable are A. N. Voronikhin (1760–1814), A. D. Zakharov (1761–1811), J. T. de Thomon (a Frenchman, 1760–1813), V. P. Stasov (1769–1848), O. I. Bove (1784–1834), K. (C.) Rossi (Russian-born of Italian origins, 1775–1849), D. Zhilyardi (or Gilardi – another second-generation immigrant, 1788–1845).

The one major public building of the nineteenth century that seems an unqualified architectural masterpiece is one of the earliest: Zakharov's remodelling of the great Admiralty in Petersburg (1806). He gave the immensely long façade and side-wings a variety of subsidiary colonnaded porticoes in Russian Palladian taste, reserving his most original effects for the central block containing the main, semi-circular portal. This is a great unfenestrated cube, dramatically adorned with large free-standing and low-relief sculptures. Above it rises a smaller cube – this one formed by an open colonnade, topped with more statues. But Zakharov's most daring and unexpected touch is to have left, rising from the centre of these two stark cubes, the slim golden spire with which Korobov had crowned Peter the Great's first Admiralty in his reconstruction of 1732. This notable landmark adds a touch of fancifulness to a building which, for all its vastness, neither oppresses nor dominates the city-scape. The Admiralty, and Zakharov's lesser buildings (the chief of which is the cathedral in Kronstadt, 1806), show that, while he was attracted by the uningratiating though impressive geometricity characteristic particularly of later French Neo-Classical architecture, he could temper its starkness – even brutality – with graceful touches that witness to the native eighteenth-century tradition. The spare forms of late European Neo-Classicism, their inspiration regressing through the Doric order back to the 'Egyptian', thus develop in an attractive Russian variant – from Zakharov to some of Zhilyardi's structures and to Stasov's notable, laconic Victualling Stores in Moscow (1832, planned 1821).

Zakharov's direct influence is strongly manifest in the Petersburg Stock Exchange (Birzha) designed as a Doric temple by de Thomon in 1805; with its flanking Customs Stores, and the Rostral Columns in front, it forms an ensemble at the tip (*Strelka*) of Vasil'yev Island which has unsurpassed importance for the Petersburg/Leningrad townscape to this day. Another architect whose hand is felt in de Thomon's final plans is Voronikhin; his Mining Institute (1806) is, like the Birzha, notable for its severe Doric colonnade. Voronikhin's Stroganov Dacha was light and charming; but his best-known work, the Kazan' Cathedral in Petersburg (1801), is less positively successful. In it he has nonetheless made the best of the

Moscow, Kropotkin Street, showing house of Dolgorukov family (M. F. Kazakov, 1790) and Academy of Arts (early nineteenth century).

impossible task of designing a small-scale pastiche of St Peter's in Rome. Already, we feel, the eclecticism that was to undermine Russian Neo-Classicism is beginning to make itself felt in large-scale ecclesiastical architecture. St Isaac's Cathedral in Petersburg (by Montferrand, 1817 onwards), whose golden dome is a fine sight from far off, has at closer acquaintance a ponderousness and unstylishness still foreign to the domestic architecture of the time.

The last notable architect to help mould the classical Petersburg town-scape was Rossi. His finest achievement may be his last major commission: the Senate and Synod (1829). The huge range of buildings (1819) with which he closed the (Winter) Palace Square is notable for the imposing, almost threatening, double archway leading through it to the Nevsky Prospekt. His Mikhaylov Palace (nowadays housing the Russian Museum) is also huge – too huge, for a house built in the purest taste of Russian Classicism, whose effects were always most successful when they did not try to overwhelm. Its effect is imposing but cold, and the same might even be said of the short, finely proportioned and symmetrical street

St Petersburg, Admiralty main entrance (A. D. Zakharov, 1806); spire by I. Korobov (1732).

Moscow, Victualling Stores by V. P. Stasov (1832, designed 1821).

(leading to his Aleksandrinsky Theatre) which now bears Rossi's name. But his superb sense of town-planning made an important contribution to Russian architecture, and his smaller works (e.g. on Yelagin Island) and architectural detail show restraint and elegance.

These qualities are more marked in the best Moscow architecture of the time, perhaps because of its less 'official' status. Bove's Bol'shoy Theatre (1821), part of a larger complex, underwent unfortunate later restoration and modification by Kavos, and his masterpiece was the house he built for N. S. Gagarin (1817). But it is Zhilyardi who qualifies as the last really great architect of the period to work in either capital. No other architect, not even Kazakov, has so firmly left his imprint on the Classical Moscow that we know today: clearcut, bold forms with delicate moulding and low-relief friezes characterize his style. His chief public works are the reconstruction of Kazakov's Moscow University (1817, after damage in the Fire of 1812), and the splendidly elegant Wardship Council building (1825); but these are medium-sized, rather than large structures, and share the qualities of his numerous domestic buildings – of which those on the Naydyonov (1829) and Kuz'minki (1820s) estates are the most famous. Moscow contemporaries A. G. Grigor'yev (1782–1868) and Ye. D. Tyurin (1792–1870) are worthy to stand beside him; the latter's Yelokhovo Cathedral (1837) is perhaps the last important building of true Russian Neo-Classicism.

The transition to the eclectic styles so typical of the mid-nineteenth

St Petersburg, Colonnade of Kazan' Cathedral (A. N. Voronikhin, 1801).

century is seen in the work of such architects as A. P. Bryullov (1798–1877) in Petersburg and K. A. Ton (1794–1881) in Moscow. The latter's huge Cathedral of the Saviour (1837), demolished in the 1930s, was a notable and richly ornate Moscow landmark; architecturally its attempt to revive Old Russian forms appears to have been clumsy and uncomprehending. Ton's palace in the Kremlin (1838) is, of course, still one of the most prominent buildings in the city: irritating as it may seem, its pastiche

Moscow, Gagarin House on Novinsky Boulevard, central part of façade (O. I. Bove, 1817, destroyed by bombing 1941).

St Petersburg, General Staff building, arch by K. Rossi (1819).

99

detail is not without a certain cheerfulness, and the palace does not ruin its surroundings as completely as might have been feared. In much less pompous vein, Ton built the terminal stations (1851) on the Petersburg–Moscow railway in a lighthearted, more-or-less Classical manner: these highlight the fact that Neo-Classicism in its decline was still exercising a beneficial effect on minor functional and popular architecture, as a wander through the back streets of Moscow or any old provincial town will make obvious. Through this protracted lapse into the vernacular – here an unassuming pediment, there a stuccoed bas-relief or a column or two – Neo-Classicism showed that, outlasting higher changes of fashion, it had entered into the very centre of the Russian aesthetic consciousness.

Painting

That we should devote less space to painting and sculpture of the Neo-Classical period than to architecture is in the order of things: Russia's contribution in these fields was by any standards less important. Yet a handful of the greatest artists have a European significance equal to that of the architects. Foremost among them are the two painters born in the 1730s, Levitsky and Rokotov, whom we mentioned earlier.

Of these D. G. Levitsky (1735–1822) has always been the better known. His father was an engraver; he trained in Kiev under Antropov, who was realizing the decoration of Rastrelli's great Church of St Andrew during the 1750s. He first exhibited in 1770 in Petersburg, and throughout the seventies and eighties produced a series of brilliant portraits. If in an early work like the portrait of Kokorinov (1769) a certain Baroque flourish and formality still obtain, he soon cultivated the quiet insight and concern for the subtleties of personality which are characteristic of the best portraiture of the neo-Classical period. Diderot owned, and particularly valued, the famous small painting which Levitsky did of him in 1773–4. His female portraits have charm, and those of a number of Smol'ny schoolgirls a delightful picturesqueness. In painting Catherine

Moscow, Kuz'minki estate (D. Zhilyardi, 1820s).

he showed he could adopt a somewhat grander manner. His draughts-manship was impeccable, and his colour-sense particularly outstanding.

By contrast F. S. Rokotov (1735–1808) is a more limited artist; that is to say he imposed limits on himself. For after his return to Moscow from Petersburg in 1765 he concentrated more and more exclusively on a certain type of portrait, which he made completely, and unmistakably, his own. This was a development away (as with Levitsky) from any remnants of Baroque attitudes, and it led Rokotov into the unassuming genre of the 'chamber portrait' (often oval in shape), where all the interest is concentrated on the subtlety, even ambiguity, of the sitter's features. Background is disregarded, only the head and shoulders have prominence, and even they are no more than a framework for the all important facial expression. Rokotov achieves these effects through a 'melting' technique, suggesting indirect and subdued lighting, relying on the finest modelling more than on draughtsmanship. The typical eighteenth-century 'half-smile' grows with Rokotov to dominate a portrait such as that of Maykov (c. 1765), as the eyes do in that of Struyskaya (1772), and the quiet intensity achieved by such means is almost uncanny. Rokotov did not lack commissions in his lifetime, but after his death fell into oblivion (even more than the other painters of his century); his 'rediscovery' after a hundred years of neglect has been followed by steadily growing appreciation and investigation, to the point where he is surely to be regarded as one of the most individual, perhaps greatest, figures in the arts of eighteenth-century Russia.

D. G. Levitsky, 'Catherine II' (1783).   F. S. Rokotov, 'A. P. Struyskaya' (1772).

101

To reach the third great Russian portraitist of the age we move forward a generation. V. L. Borovikovsky (1757–1825) was a native of the Ukraine, like Levitsky, and like him was the son of an artist; he probably studied with him when he came to Petersburg, where most of his work was done. The proto-Romantic 'sentimentalism' (not incompatible with Classicism) that affected European art and literature in the later eighteenth century found, perhaps, its best pictorial expression in Russia with Borovikovsky's work of the 1790s. Again like his great predecessors he is a master of the female portrait; his famous picture of M. I. Lopukhina (1797) is charged with sensuous brilliance, and the smouldering gaze of his sitter is, typically, enhanced by a touch of evocative landscape in the background. With sentimentalism came informality in the treatment of high subjects, and two of the best-known of Borovikovsky's pictures depict Catherine the Great as a comfortable matriarch, strolling in her park.

It is interesting that portraiture, so typically Russian an art-form, continues to produce the finest works of easel-painting even during the Europeanized age of Enlightenment Classicism. But other genres – historical, narrative, landscape – begin to flourish in Russia at this time, even though the results achieved are less impressive. Worthy of mention is the founder of Russian historical painting, A. P. Losenko (1737–73), another Ukrainian, whose 'Vladimir and Rogneda' (1770) achieved

V. L. Borovikovsky, 'M. I. Lopukhina' (1797).

O. A. Kiprensky, 'Alexander Pushkin' (1827).

lasting success. Nowadays we are likely to regard him more highly in his role as a most skilful draughtsman and teacher. After his early death G. I. Ugryumov (1764–1823) developed historical painting further. The origins of Russian genre painting can be found in the work of M. Shibanov and the curious, little-investigated I. Yermenyov. Landscape (and townscape) had been more strongly developed from an earlier period. In Peter the Great's day A. F. Zubov (1682–1744) had produced attractive engravings of the new city. M. I. Makhayev's (1716–70) similar engravings are also noteworthy; while Russian topographical painting reaches its highest point with the work of S. F. Shchedrin (1745–94) and particularly F. Ya. Alekseyev (1753–1824).

The early nineteenth century saw a flush of Russian painters, in few of whom talent really matched pretensions. The greatest are probably the genre-painter A. G. Venetsianov (1780–1847) and the portraitist O. A. Kiprensky (1782–1836). Both, in different ways, feel the breath of the Romantic movement. But in Russia this movement, whether in art or literature, did not have quite the same significance as it had in western European countries: its impact is softer, and more integrated into the general atmosphere of the Enlightenment. Particularly characteristic of this spirit is Kiprensky's memorable portrait of the writer Alexander Pushkin (1827), whose own role in Russian culture sums up these ambiguously Classic/Romantic tendencies: it has a humane *gravitas* which does

F. Ya. Alekseyev, 'Stock Exchange', St Petersburg (1810).

A. G. Venetsianov, 'Threshing-floor' (1821).

K. P. Bryullov, 'The Last Day of Pompeii' (1833).

not exclude a measure of subdued tension. Kiprensky's earlier works are closer to the 'intimate portrait' tradition of the eighteenth century, though with more recognizably Romantic touches and an admirable freedom of line. Venetsianov too began as a painter of 'intimate portraits' (under the influence of Borovikovsky). These two masters, in fact, mark the final stage of a tradition which had sprung from Rokotov's works of the 1760s; both abandoned it in the 1820s. Venetsianov is best remembered today for his later works: mostly genre scenes set in peasant Russia, they have a spaciousness, a quality of light and an unpretentious subtlety which mark him out as a truly original artist.

P. A. Fedotov, 'Officer and Orderly' (*c.* 1850).

A similar degree of taste informs the work of one or two other artists of the time: worthy of note are the portraits of V. A. Tropinin (1776–1857), and the versatile F. P. Tolstoy (1783–1873) who – better known for his bas-relief sculpture – was also a notable draughtsman, in a manner recalling Flaxman's work. But in the case of several better-known names taste is precisely what is lacking. It is strange to recollect that K. P. Bryullov (1799–1852) and A. A. Ivanov (1806–58) are the contemporaries of Pushkin or Glinka, and in their time seemed to hold an equally import-ant place in Russian culture. Both spent the chief working years of their lives in Italy, and made something of a name for themselves in European circles: Bryullov's grandest painting, 'The Last Day of Pompeii' (1833), was the direct inspiration for Bulwer-Lytton's famous novel. Bryullov was in fact an artist of considerable vitality and inventiveness, whose work too often teetered on the edge of the ridiculous: many will consider that 'The Last Day' has crossed this brink. Ivanov – a very different artistic personality – devoted most of his life to a single large painting, 'The Appearance of Christ to the People' (1837–57). Not surprisingly the result (never quite finished) is over-studied and cold, for all the seriousness and sincerity which he brought to his task. In Russia it has always been highly esteemed, and still is; possibly more for the moral qualities in Ivanov which so attracted Gogol and Tolstoy than for its intrinsic merits. It brought something new into Russian art, but that something owed too much to the German 'Nazarene' community close to whom Ivanov lived. The numerous studies and sketches he made for his *magnum opus* may well interest us more than the work itself.

With lesser artists such as F. A. Bruni – painter of coldly Classical historical canvases – I. K. Ayvazovsky (1817–1900), whose seascapes follow a long way after Turner, and P. A. Fedotov (1815–52) – much the most interesting of the three, who produced satirical genre scenes often compared, though rather unconvincingly, with Hogarth's – we reach the mid-nineteenth century, and a moment when the incipient contradic-tions in the development of Russian art come to a head, with surprising and profound results.

Sculpture

Of the other arts in Russia during the Neo-Classical period, sculpture holds first place. Russia produced one master of European quality – F. I. Shubin (1740–1805) – and several figures of local importance. Shubin's marble portrait-busts have outstanding expressiveness and feeling for his material; their strong characterization avoids Rococo coyness or Baroque lavishness on the one hand, and on the other the coldness that often infects even the best-known Neo-Classical sculptors of western Europe; he is not unworthy to stand beside the great Houdon. Like many of the

F. I. Shubin, 'Emperor Paul', marble (1797).

leading artists of eighteenth-century Russia, he was of humble birth, and grew up (as we mentioned earlier) among peasant wood-carvers on the White Sea coast. This was the milieu which produced the great Lomonosov, whom (after his death) Shubin sculpted in one of his best works (1792). Perhaps his most unforgettable portraits are those of the ugly, stubborn, ill-fated Tsar Paul (1796–1801). Other worthwhile sculptors of the period include I. P. Prokof'yev, F. F. Shchedrin, and the more ambitious M. I. Kozlovsky (1753–1802), whose monumental works (notably the memorial to Suvorov, 1802) strain a little too hard for effect. I. P. Martos (1754–1835), probably the best Russian sculptor after Shubin, is similarly less impressive in his prominently situated monument to Minin and Pozharsky (in Red Square, Moscow) than in his many delicate tomb monuments, architectural reliefs and other smaller-scale works. Classical sculpture ends, by no means ignominiously, with the work of such artists as F. P. Tolstoy (mentioned earlier), I. P. Vitali (1794–1855) and Baron P. K. Klodt (1805–67), whose four cheerful horses at each corner of the Anichkov Bridge in Petersburg are so famous a landmark to this day. But the greatest single piece of sculpture in Russia – probably the finest equestrian statue of modern times – is the

Foreground: Monument to Peter the Great: the 'Bronze Horseman' (E.-M. Falconet, completed 1782), overlooking present-day Leningrad, towards Vasil'-yev Island and 'Petersburg side' across the Bol'shaya Neva. *Left to right* (principal buildings only): end of 'Twelve Colleges' (D. Trezzini, 1721); Academy of Sciences (G. Quarenghi, 1783); Kunstkamera (J. Mattarnovi and M. Zemtsov, 1718); Rostral Column (T. de Thomon, 1805); Cathedral of SS Peter and Paul (D. Trezzini, 1712).

work of a Frenchman who did not settle permanently in the country: E.-M. Falconet's statue of Peter the Great, known universally, after Pushkin, as the 'Bronze Horseman' (started in 1766, completed in 1782). Its daring effect depends more than anything on the enormous block of granite – not reproducing, but suggesting a breaking wave – above which rears the horse with its rider. That the potential for a single mighty work like this was realized in Falconet, known previously as a producer of charming Rococo figurines, is a tribute to Diderot (who recommended him to Catherine II), and to Russia, for inspiring him to so splendid a vision, and giving him – not without difficulties – the means to achieve it.

GUIDE TO FURTHER READING

General works on Russian art and architecture, 988–1860

There are several general studies of Russian art and architecture available in English, but none so far takes adequate account of recent scholarship, and all are marred by errors of detail. The fullest and thus most useful is G. H. Hamilton, *Art and Architecture of Russia* (Harmondsworth, 2nd edn, 1975). T. Talbot Rice, *A Concise History of Russian Art* (London, 1963) is copiously illustrated. The brief account by M. Chamot, *Russian Painting and Sculpture* (Oxford, 1963) deals mostly with nineteenth-century painting. A somewhat dated, but unusual and still valuable study (particularly on the eighteenth century) is M. Alpatov, *The Russian Impact on Art* (2nd ed., New York, 1969). There are some useful articles in the multi-volume *Encyclopaedia of World Art* (New York, 1959 onwards): see particularly under *Union of Soviet Socialist Republics.* Several books which are primarily picture-albums are also useful for their text: *Arts of Russia* (Geneva, 1964), vol. I ed. by K. Kornilovich, vol. II by A. Kaganovich; T. Copplestone (ed.), *Art Treasures in Russia* (London, 1971); M. Alpatov, *Art Treasures of Russia* (2nd ed., London, 1975). There are many articles on Russian subjects in the *Penguin Dictionary of Architecture* (Harmondsworth, 1966 etc.); note also K. Berton, *Moscow: An Architectural History* (London, 1976). The only adequate critical guide to the extant monuments and museums is in German: E. Behrens, *Kunst in Russland* (Cologne, 1969). Most western accounts of Russian art stand in excessive debt to the weighty but outdated works of L. Réau: *L'Art russe des origines à Pierre le Grand* (Paris, 1921) and *L'Art russe de Pierre le Grand à nos jours* (Paris, 1922).

The basic Russian-language work of reference is the multi-volume *Istoriya russkogo iskusstva*, ed. I. Grabar' *et al.* (Moscow–Leningrad, 1940–). Convenient brief histories are A. L. Kaganovich (ed.), *Istoriya russkogo iskusstva* (Moscow, 1961) and A. I. Zotov, *Russkoye iskusstvo* (Moscow, 1971). For architecture, see S. V. Bezsonov *et al.*, *Istoriya russkoy arkhitektury* (Moscow, 1951; 2nd ed., 1956) and V. H. Zabolotny *et al.*, *Narysy istorii arkhitektury Ukrain'skoy RSR* (Kiev, 1957).

Complementary and background works

There are several commendable introductions in English to the world of Byzantine and Orthodox art in general: e.g. A. Grabar, *Byzantium*, in the series *Arts of the World* (London, 1966) and G. Mathew, *Byzantine Aesthetics* (London, 1963). Other important background works which help to integrate Old Russian art into its cultural–historical milieu include D. Obolensky, *The Byzantine Commonwealth* (London, 1971), T. Ware,

The Orthodox Church (Harmondsworth, 1963) and G. Fedotov, *The Russian Religious Mind*, 2 vols. (Cambridge, Mass., 1966). In Russian, D. Likhachev (ed.), *Kul'tura drevney Rusi* (Moscow, 1967), A. Artsikhovsky (ed.), *Ocherki russkoy kul'tury XII–XV vekov*, part 2 (Moscow, 1960), D. Likhachev, *Kul'tura Rusi vremeni A. Rublyova i Epifaniya Premudrogo* (Leningrad, 1962; also in German translation, Dresden, 1962), V. and D. Likhachev, *Khudozhestvennoye naslediye drevney Rusi i sovremennost'* (Leningrad, 1971) and the volume in the annual series *Trudy Otdela drevnerusskoy literatury* devoted to *Vzaimodeystviye literatury i izobrazitel'nogo iskusstva v drevney Rusi* (XXII, Moscow–Leningrad, 1966).

Specialist studies, 988–1700

Few studies of particular areas within the field of Old Russian art and architecture have appeared in English. Far the most important are V. Lazarev, *Old Russian Murals and Mosaics* (London, 1966), which not only deals exhaustively with Russian wall-painting up to *c*. 1500, but gives an authoritative account of the methods of work of Old Russian artists, and H. Faensen and V. Ivanov, *Early Russian Architecture* (London, 1975) – detailed and copiously illustrated. There is no comparable study of icon-painting in English, though albums such as *USSR: Early Russian Icons* (UNESCO, 1958), V. Lazarev, *Novgorodian Icon Painting* (Moscow, 1969) and K. Onasch, *Icons* (London, 1963) can be recommended. O. Popova, *Les Miniatures russes du XIe au XVe siècle* (Leningrad, 1975) is reliable and well illustrated.

In Russian, the field is wide. Of great importance are all volumes in the occasional series edited by V. Lazarev *et al.* under the general title *Drevnerusskoye iskusstvo* (Moscow, 1963–), dealing (e.g.) with: the fifteenth to early sixteenth centuries; the seventeenth century; Novgorod; Pskov; early Moscow. All are miscellanies of scholarly articles by various authors. Lazarev has himself written such monographs as *Freski Staroy Ladogi* (Moscow, 1960), *Feofan Grek i yego shkola* (Moscow, 1961) and the best book on Rublyov: *Andrey Rublyov i yego shkola* (Moscow, 1966); a collection of his articles has appeared under the title *Russkaya srednevekovaya zhivopis'* (Moscow, 1970). The (usually) annual volumes of *Arkhitekturnoye nasledstvo* have contained much of the most important recent research into Old Russian (and later) architecture. An admirable and exhaustive study is N. Voronin, *Zodchestvo severo-vostochnoy Rusi* (2 vols., Moscow, 1962). The series of small architectural guides to Russian cities from the publishing house Iskusstvo (Moscow) maintains a consistently high standard of scholarship and presentation: note particularly the volumes covering Moscow (by M. Il'yin), Vladimir etc. (N. Voronin), Novgorod (M. Karger), Chernigov etc. (G. Logvin), Vologda etc. (G. Bocharov and V. Vygolov); some have been translated into English. On sculpture and the minor arts, note in particular G. Vagner, *Skul'ptura drevney Rusi – XII v.* (Moscow, 1969) on Vladimir–Suzdal' carving; N. Pomerantsev, *Russkaya derevyannaya skul'ptura* (Moscow, 1967); and T. Nikolayeva, *Drevnerusskaya melkaya plastika XI–XVI vekov* (Moscow, 1968). Many Russian-language specialist studies nowadays contain an English summary of the text.

Specialist studies, 1700–1860

There is little of value in English on the art of Petersburg Russia; reference must be made to the works listed under *General works*, particularly *Arts of Russia*, vol. II. On the cultural background, see J. G. Garrard (ed.), *The Eighteenth Century in Russia* (Oxford, 1973), with article on art by T. Talbot Rice. Some recent Soviet albums have an English as well as a Russian text: e.g. K. Mikhaylova, *Rokotov* (Masters of World Painting series,

Leningrad, 1971). Many scholarly volumes in Russian treat individual aspects of the art of the period: e.g. T. Alekseyeva (ed.), *Russkoye iskusstvo XVIII veka* (Moscow, 1968); I. Grabar' (ed.), *Russkaya arkhitektura pervoy poloviny XVIII v.* (Moscow, 1954); and N. Kovalenskaya, *Russkiy klassitsizm* (Moscow, 1964); M. Rakova, *Russkoye iskusstvo pervoy poloviny XIX v.* (Moscow, 1975) is concise and well illustrated. There are reliable Russian monographs on all the main painters, sculptors and architects of the time; they are too numerous to list (in general, the more recent the better). On architecture and town-planning see *Istoriya russkoy arkhitektury* and other works listed under *General works*, and the series of guides to individual cities in the last section; to the ones listed there may be added those to Leningrad (by V. Shvarts) and the Podmoskov'ye (by M. Il'yin). A useful album with English text is N. Gosling, *Leningrad* (London, 1965); a more comprehensive Soviet album is N. N. Belekhova, *Pamyatniki arkhitektury Leningrada* (Leningrad, 1958). On the minor arts see (e.g. Yu. Ovsyannikov, *The Lubok* (Moscow, 1968) and T. Goldberg (ed.), *Russkoye zolotoye i serebryannoye delo XV–XX vekov* (Moscow, 1967).

3

ART AND ARCHITECTURE IN THE AGE OF REVOLUTION, 1860–1917

Art

The 1850s marked a significant turning-point in the history of the Imperial Academy, for this august institution now felt the first overt symptoms of active revolt against its teachings, with the result that its artistic and material hegemony became seriously threatened. The mounting discontent with the Academy's concentration on Classical models, totally divorced from contemporary reality, reached a climax in 1863 with the famous revolt of the fourteen students – thirteen painters and one sculptor – led by I. N. Kramskoy (1837–87). The formal occasion for their action was the stipulation of a mythological subject for the historical section of the annual Gold Medal competition – 'The Feast of the Gods in Valhalla'; the group of radicals refused to paint a theme which was so irrelevant to the social needs of the day and as a mark of their discontent resigned *en masse* from the Academy. However, in the genre section of the Competition a subject which was topical and socially tendentious was offered simultaneously – 'The Liberation of the Serfs'. One must therefore regard the revolt not as the outcome of mere dissatisfaction with a specific title, but as the result of a combination of circumstances, as the climax to a decade of tension. The real causes of the revolt are to be seen not simply in the revolutionary fervour of the young generation of Academy students, but also in the direct influence of the more flexible and progressive teaching system at the Moscow Institute of Painting and Sculpture[1] and in the extensive propagation of the new socio-political and aesthetic ideas of Chernyshevsky and Dobrolyubov. The immediate effect of the uprising was twofold: it presented a serious threat to the autocracy of the Academy, which thereafter entered a state of distinct decline at least until its partial reformation in the early 1890s, and it introduced to Russian art new artists and a new artistic direction – Realism.

[1] Ever since its foundation in 1832 the Moscow Institute of Painting and Sculpture had been a more progressive establishment both in its teaching staff and in its student population. A Department of Architecture was added in 1865.

Even before 1863 a few artists, especially V. G. Perov (1833–82), had been acutely aware of the problems in Russian society and had sought to reflect in their canvases such issues as the poverty of the peasants or the corruption of the Church (see, for example, Perov's 'Easter Procession in the Country', 1861, TG[2]). Moreover, such artists had been in close contact with progressive writers, musicians and thinkers of the time, a tradition which the new Realists were quick to maintain. One of the results of this association was a whole series of interesting portraits (e.g. Perov's of Dostoyevsky, 1872, TG; Kramskoy's of Tolstoy, 1873, TG; Repin's of Stasov, 1883, RM[3] and of Musorgsky, 1881, TG). While these often suffered from photographic naturalism (it is significant that Kramskoy worked at one time as a retoucher), they were, for the most part, incisive records of leading contemporaries, and formed possibly the greatest artistic achievement of the Realist painters.

Although the fourteen artists soon attracted new colleagues, they did not become a formal, titled group until 1870 when they organized the so-called 'Society of Wandering Exhibitions' and hence took the name of

Vasily Perov, 'Easter Procession in the Country' (1861).

[2] TG = Tret'yakov Gallery, Moscow.
[3] RM = Russian Museum, Leningrad.

'Wanderers' (*Peredvizhniki*). From 1871 until 1918, and again briefly in the early 1920s, they held regular exhibitions, although by the early 1890s these had become synonymous with hackwork and weak technique. Although the group issued no independent manifesto, it became immediately apparent that some of them followed the principles of Perov and tended to view art as a vehicle for social criticism and improvement. Perhaps the most important of the Wanderers was their unfailing champion, I. Ye. Repin (1844–1930), whose tendentious scenes such as the 'Bargemen'

Il'ya Repin, 'Portrait of the Composer Modest Musorgsky' (1881).

(known as the 'Volga Boatmen', 1870, RM) and 'They Did Not Expect Him' (1884, TG) were technically good, if not always thematically profound; in addition, such pictures typified the Realist structural approach with their emphasis on a central diagonal line such as a procession – to afford mobility and communication between all planes of the picture – and their deliberate gestures and actions orientated to a world outside the frame.

Repin also became famous for his portraits of intellectuals of the day such as Tolstoy (1887, TG and elsewhere) and Musorgsky (1881, TG), which tended to reflect his uneven style: in fact, he exemplified the whole development of Realism in the visual arts, for while starting in the late 1860s as a revolutionary and innovatory artist, he descended into monotonous naturalism, tending to question or even condemn the discoveries of later unorthodox groups such as the 'World of Art' and the 'Blue Rose'. During the 1870s, however, Repin and his confrères dominated the artistic arena, thanks not only to their own activity, but also to the spiritual and ideological support from the leading critic of that decade, V. V. Stasov (1824–1906): his numerous articles and exhibition reviews helped to disseminate the new artistic credo and to propagate the painting of such Wanderers as N. N. Ge (1831–94), I. I. Shishkin (1832–98), V. I. Surikov (1848–1916) and, specifically, the celebrated battle-painter, V. V. Vereshchagin (1842–1904), who, although never exhibiting at the Wanderers' exhibitions, was an undoubted supporter of their world-view. Like Repin, however, Stasov failed to respond to the aesthetic innovations of the early 1900s and condemned them without mitigation. The Wanderers relied also for their success on the extensive purchases by one of Russia's greatest bourgeois art patrons, P. M. Tret'yakov (1832–98), who collected canvases of all the main Realists – and it was his private collection, given to the Moscow public in 1892, which came to form the basis of the holdings of the present Tret'yakov Gallery.

While undoubtedly injecting new vigour into Russian painting after the stagnation of the 1840s and 1850s, the Wanderers deserve to be remembered as a vital testing-ground for young, unrecognized talents. Their yearly exhibitions attracted many future masters including K. A. Korovin (1861–1939), I. I. Levitan (1860–1900), M. V. Nesterov (1862–1942), V. A. Serov (1865–1911) and the Vasnetsov brothers, V. M. (1848–1926) and A. M. (1856–1933). Indeed, it was these artists who, while appreciating the achievements of the Wanderers, added a formal and thematic flexibility which, by the 1880s, was long overdue. In this respect, Levitan's contribution to the Russian school of landscape painting is of profound significance, while Serov's work in portraiture and the domestic genre exerted a definite influence on the new generation of the 1900s. Yet by the 1880s the original Wanderers had, for the most part, lost their artistic vitality as their once trenchant canvases gave way to sentimental landscapes and domestic scenes.

One of the consequences of the reaction against the Academy had been the subsequent neglect of technique, and this became especially manifest in the works of S. V. Ivanov (1864–1910), N. A. Klodt (1865–1918) and other epigones of Realism. At the same time peasant art was being threatened – not merely by weak technique or sentimentalization of subject, but by the pernicious effects of industry. The intense process of urbanization which Russia was then undergoing meant that peasants flocked to the towns, abandoning their traditional domestic arts and crafts: their hand-made wood-carvings, fabrics and icons began to be superseded by factory-produced items and, as a direct result, a whole cultural heritage was suddenly faced with extinction.

Certainly, some of the Wanderers, particularly V. D. Polenov (1844–1927), Repin, Surikov and V. Vasnetsov, focused attention on peasant costume and artifacts in their pictures, but this was only a gesture of appreciation and did little to improve the situation in concrete terms. Fortunately, there were some who were aware both of the imminent loss of traditional art forms and of the spiritual impasse which easel painting was entering and who endeavoured in a practical way to overcome these problems. For the most part they belonged to that very class whose activities were contributing to the decline of peasant art – industrialists and wealthy aristocrats; chief among these were S. I. Mamontov (1841–1918) and Princess M. K. Tenisheva (Ténicheff, 1867–1928), figures who must at least be mentioned in any examination of Modernist Russian art.

Of the two Mamontov was the more powerful and influential, although the achievements of Princess Tenisheva should by no means be forgotten. In 1870 Mamontov bought an estate called Abramtsevo, not far from Moscow, and it was there that the famous artists' colony of that name was established. Mamontov was deeply interested in peasant art, both Russian and western European, and was familiar with the tenets of William Morris. His artistic interests widened when he made the acquaintance of Polenov, Repin and V. Vasnetsov who, among others, came to work at Abramtsevo in the late 1870s. By 1880 a distinct artistic collective had been formed there, united ideologically by a mutual interest in the history of Russian culture, in landscape painting and by a critical attitude towards the later sentimentalism of the Wanderers. With the establishment of studios and workshops, there began a period of intense artistic creativity which was to continue at Abramtsevo for at least the next decade. Apart from easel paintings and sculptures, artists turned their attention to the design of furniture, utensils and embroidery, based on

Yelena Polenova, illustration to *The Fire-bird* (1900).

traditional, peasant motifs, and the resultant style, known as the Neo-nationalist or Russian Style, was perpetuated by such artists as K. Korovin, Ye. D. Polenova (1850–98), V. Vasnetsov, M. A. Vrubel' (1856–1910) and M. V. Yakunchikova (1870–1902). Elements of Neo-nationalism were carried over into other art forms such as book illustration and stage decoration, and it is in the initial sets designed by such artists as K. Korovin and Vrubel' for Mamontov's Private Opera (founded in 1885) that one can trace the genesis of the upsurge of decorative art identified with Diaghilev and the 'World of Art' in the 1900s.

Princess Tenisheva established a similar art colony called Talashkino on her estate near Smolensk. Although Talashkino did not enjoy artistic success at least until the late 1890s, its aims were similar to those of Abramtsevo. Important artists worked there, including A. Ya. Golovin (1863–1930), S. V. Malyutin (1859–1937), N. K. Rerikh (Roerich, 1874–1947) and Vrubel', who produced numerous examples of Neo-nationalist art. It can be argued, even, that the furniture, embroidery and wood-carving modelled at Talashkino according to traditional patterns were, perhaps, intrinsically more genuine than the parallel output of Abramtsevo, even though, for example, the heavy ornamentation of Malyutin's work rendered his chairs and tables quite unpractical. But although the stylization and features of Art Nouveau which affected many of the Abramtsevo artifacts were far less obtrusive in the Talashkino wares, and although Talashkino was enjoying an international reputation in the early 1900s, the enterprise entered a rapid state of decline after 1905.

Perhaps the greatest of the artists associated with both Abramtsevo and Talashkino was Vrubel'. Although he worked in painting and in sculpture, his most original works were his monumental canvases based on historical and legendary subjects. His powerful imagination was well reflected in such large pictures as 'Pan' (1899, TG) and 'Demon Downcast' (1902, TG) and in the series of mythological panneaux for A. V. Morozov's villa in Moscow (1896–8). While Art Nouveau and Neo-nationalism are terms which come to mind in the context of Vrubel''s work, his individuality always left its imprint, even in his small-scale graphic works, such as his illustrations to Lermontov's *Demon*. His distinctive originality was manifest, above all, in his fragmentary approach to the pictorial surface and it is significant, therefore, that later a leading critic should have referred to Vrubel' in the context of Cubism,[4] for Vrubel''s 'broken' brushwork strangely anticipated the visual dislocation of the late 1900s. In this respect, he forms one of the vital links between the Realism of the 1870s and the first leftist currents of the early 1900s.

[4] S. Makovsky, 'Vrubel' i Rerikh', in *Siluety russkikh khudozhnikov*, Prague, 1922, pp. 110–32.

By the late 1890s a group of artists, aesthetes and critics had come together in St Petersburg, united in their hostility towards both the Academy and the Wanderers. Led at first by A. N. Benois (1870–1960) and the writer D. V. Filosofov (1872–1940), they had been joined in 1890 by S. P. Diaghilev (1872–1929) who eight years later welded the group into the 'World of Art' (*Mir iskusstva*): it was this circle of young men which launched the famous magazine of that name (1898–1904), organized a series of highly important exhibitions, and propagated Russian art and music so successfully in the west.

The 'World of Art' artists never issued a written manifesto, but it would be fair to summarize their credo as 'art for art's sake', and their attention to artistic craft, their cult of retrospective beauty and their neglect of socio-political issues linked them immediately with the Russian Symbolist writers, especially the so-called first generation, many of whom frequented their meetings. The major figures of the initial group, L. S. Bakst (1866–1924), Benois, Ye. Ye. Lansere (1875–1946), A. P. Ostroumova-Lebedeva (1871–1955), Serov and K. A. Somov (1869–1939), not to mention later members such as I. Ya. Bilibin (1876–1942) and M. V. Dobuzhinsky (1875–1957), shared, above all, the desire to recapture that formal discipline which had been lost after the technical laxity of the Wanderers. Thus we find that some of the greatest achievements of the 'World of Art' painters are to be seen in those art forms which dictate intensive concentration of line and extraordinary finesse – the miniature, the silhouette, book illustration and diminutive water-colours and pastels. This is not to say, of course, that they ignored other areas of painting: Somov produced some remarkable portraits of his contemporaries, such as the poet Blok (1906, TG); so did Bakst, in his portraits of Andrey Bely (1905, Moscow Literary Museum, later version in Ashmolean, Oxford) and Zinaida Gippius (1906, TG); and most members were fine landscapists. The fame of several 'World of Art' painters, particularly Bakst and Benois, rests, at least in the west, on their set and costume designs for Diaghilev's 'Ballets Russes' (1909–29), but while

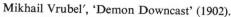

Mikhail Vrubel', 'Demon Downcast' (1902).

Lev Bakst, 'Portrait of the Writer Andrey Bely' (*c.* 1906).

Alexandre Benois, 'Décor for Armide's Garden'. For *Le Pavillon d'Armide*, ballet produced by Sergey Diaghilev, Paris (1909).

such works as Benois' décor for *Petrouchka* (Paris, 1911) deserve praise, they should not overshadow the earlier and contemporaneous easel paintings of these artists: in fact, it was not until the early 1900s that the stage became an outlet for their artistic talents and even thereafter some of the 'World of Art' painters, like Somov, virtually ignored this area of activity. Nevertheless, the ease with which such artists as Bakst, Benois, Bilibin and Rerikh transferred their pictorial ideas from easel painting to décor was indicative of the tendency towards structuralization or 'theatralization' which was evident in the bulk of their work. While their love of line and form was nurtured by their cultivation of craftsmanship and by their deep interest in the 'rational' culture of eighteenth-century France (demonstrated so well, for example, in Benois' scenes of Versailles), it was also very much a product of the *Zeitgeist* of intense aesthetic sensibility: the familiarity of the 'World of Art' with the Neo-nationalism of Abramtsevo and Talashkino and the stylization of Beardsley and the German Simplicissimus group contributed undoubtedly to their artistic development specifically in the decorative and illustrative arts.

As a group the 'World of Art' merits attention in other spheres besides those of easel painting and décor. Diaghilev, although not a painter, was a perceptive critic and an indefatigable organizer, and it was thanks mainly to his efforts that the group's magazine was financed (initially by Mamontov and Tenisheva) and that the first series of 'World of Art' exhibitions was inaugurated (1899–1906).[5] These two enterprises fulfilled the double function of propagating Russian art at home and abroad and of presenting a comprehensive survey of modern western art to the Russian public for the first time. In passing, it might be noted, however, that the 'World of Art' painters were not particularly impressed by the discoveries of the French Impressionists, regarding them in some cases as pernicious and unaesthetic.[6] Diaghilev's critical and organizational abilities were proven by his important monograph on Levitsky as well as by several articles in journals; in this area he was joined by Benois who contributed numerous articles and reviews to journals and newspapers of the 1900s and who wrote several books which even today serve as principal sources.

---

[5] Diaghilev was the organizer of several other exhibitions outside the 'World of Art' series, e.g. the exhibitions in St Petersburg of German and English watercolourists and of Scandinavian paintings (both 1897), of Russian and Finnish artists (1898), the Tauride Palace exhibition of Russian portraits (1905) and the Russian section at the Salon d'automne, Paris, 1906.

[6] See, for example, A. Benois, 'Beseda khudozhnika', in *Mir iskusstva*, 1899, no. 3/4, Khronika, p. 17.

As Diaghilev turned increasingly westward, the 'World of Art' as a group came to lose its unity of purpose. As early as 1903 there was an internal rift when Filosofov, D. S. Merezhkovsky (1866–1941) and Gippius left the editorial board to found their own literary/philosophical organ, *New Path* (*Novyy put'*, 1903/4). In 1904 the *World of Art* magazine ceased publication and in 1906 the last exhibition of the series closed; with that the group disintegrated as a single, cohesive unit. However, the 'World of Art', in name at least, but with a rather different composition, was resurrected in 1910 primarily as an exhibition society, and it continued to do valuable work in this field until it was disbanded in 1924. The dissolution of the 'World of Art' group in 1906 reflected not only an inner crisis, but also the effect of vigorous artistic competition from Moscow and the provinces: it was from this date onwards that as a centre of the artistic *avant-garde* Moscow assumed decisive importance.

Parallel to the emergence and development of the 'World of Art' in St Petersburg, an artist had been living and working in Saratov, a small town to the south of Moscow. This was V. E. Borisov-Musatov (1870–1905) who, together with Vrubel', constituted one of the most profound influences on the evolution of the Russian *avant-garde*. Impressed by Puvis de Chavannes and the Nabis (especially Maurice Denis) when he was in Paris (1895–7), he incorporated their monumentalism and subdued

Viktor Borisov-Musatov, 'Gobelin' (1901).

colours into his depictions of early nineteenth-century Russian estates inhabited by elusive, wraith-like women. In contrast to the rigid linearity and architectonics of the 'World of Art' painters, Borisov-Musatov presented a formal flexibility which did much to loosen Russian painting from the severe discipline both of the Academy and of the 'World of Art': as early as 1895 his work was described, albeit in negative terms, as '. . . morbid illusion . . . a mere mass of rough blots with no outline at all'.[7] Despite his decorative tendencies, Borisov-Musatov was an easel-painter above all and concentrated on the purely painterly elements of colour, mass and texture. In his cult of retrospectivism, in his nostalgic scenes of a more peaceful, more cohesive age, he did, of course, share the Symbolists,

Nikolay Sapunov, cover to the catalogue of the 'Blue Rose' exhibition (March/April 1907).

[7] The critic was a certain A.S. reviewing the exhibition of works by students of the Moscow Institute. See *Moskovskiy listok*, 1895, no. 7. Quoted from A. Rusakova, *V. E. Borisov-Musatov*, Leningrad–Moscow, 1966, p. 30.

wish to escape from their 'hysterical, spiritually tormented time',[8] and one of his central motifs, Woman, aligned him with such poets as Bely and Blok in their worship of the Eternal Feminine. The years immediately after 1900 marked the zenith of his artistic career. It was during this time that he created such works as 'Gobelin' (1901, TG), 'Reservoir' (1902, TG) and 'The Emerald Necklace' (1903/4, TG) which, with their illusive depictions of feminine grace, recall directly Blok's early verse to the 'Beautiful Lady'. The spectral figures, shimmering water and elusive foliage executed in pale tones of blue, green and grey which haunted Borisov-Musatov's pictures undermined the stability of visual reality – and it was the artists of the 'Blue Rose' group who adopted this tendency and developed it almost to the point of abstraction. Indeed, the importance of Borisov-Musatov lies not only in his close association with the literary Symbolist movement, but also in his establishment of a short-lived, but crucial 'school' of painters, for he was the direct instigator of the 'Blue Rose' movement, which could be regarded as the real beginning of the *avant-garde* in Russian art.

In May 1904 an untitled group of artists, for the most part students at the Moscow Institute of Painting, Sculpture and Architecture, organized an exhibition called the 'Crimson Rose' (*Alaya roza*) in Saratov. The tone of the exhibition was set by the leaders of the group, P. V. Kuznetsov (1878–1968) and P. S. Utkin (1877–1934), both former pupils of Borisov-Musatov: their pictures, in the main landscapes, lacked bright colour and strict delineation, elements which were to be identifiable with the whole output of the 'Blue Rose'.[9] With the establishment of Tarovaty's journal, Art, and Ryabushinsky's Symbolist journal, the *Golden Fleece* (*Zolotoye runo*), the Moscow-Saratov group found a vehicle for the dissemination of their art. It was under the financial auspices of N. P. Ryabushinsky (1876–1951), a banker and patron, that the so-called 'Blue Rose' exhibition was organized in March/April 1907, when sixteen artists led by Kuznetsov presented their essays in pictorial Symbolism. Essentially, the group, which included such future celebrities as N. N. Sapunov (1880–1912), M. S. Sar'yan (1880–1972) and S. Yu. Sudeykin (1882–1946) and which maintained close contact with such original artists as K. S. Petrov-Vodkin (1878–1939), was a Symbolist one both in its collective aspiration to depict an ulterior reality by visual symbols and in its association with the Symbolist writers, especially those of Moscow. Thematically and

[8] A. Benois, *Istoriya russkoy zhivopisi v XIX veke*, St Petersburg, 1901–2, pp. 271–2.
[9] The name was used for the first time only at the exhibition of that name in 1907, but it is applied here to cover the group's activities during its Symbolist period, i.e. 1904–8. The origin of the name is obscure. Bryusov may have proposed the title, although it could have been a direct reference to the Romantic 'blue flower' of Novalis' novel, *Heinrich von Ofterdingen*.

stylistically their canvases recalled those of the Nabis, particularly in
their attention to subdued colour scales – an element which they assimilated and modified through their mentor, Borisov-Musatov; above all
they were concerned with the intrinsic properties of the medium, rather
than with strict mimetic representation. The escape from photographic
naturalism to an obscure reality of mystical dream, or, as one critic
commented aptly, 'the dematerialization of nature',[10] was expressed most
forcefully in the work of Kuznetsov: his 'Blue Fountain' (1905, TG), not
actually exhibited but typical of his contribution here and probably
the most famous of his Symbolist pictures, not only depicts a subjective vision, but also, perhaps more significantly, points to the artist's
deliberate neglect of formal delineation. It is this distinct trend towards

Pavel Kuznetsov, 'The Blue Fountain' (1905).

[10] S. Makovsky, 'Dematerializatsiya prirody', in *Stranitsy khudozhestvennoy kritiki*, vol.
2, St Petersburg, 1909, pp. 142–6.

non-representationalism, balanced by exquisite combinations of cold colours and contrasting textures, which is peculiar to the best work of the 'Blue Rose' and which, in turn, heralds the revolutionary conception of the picture as a self-sufficient unit.

By the end of 1907 a distinct change was noticeable in the work of Kuznetsov and his colleagues, caused as much by their own maturation as by extrinsic factors. Kuznetsov's canvases of late 1907 to 1909 reflect an intense despair, a disillusionment in Symbolism as a positive world-view, and, like the contemporaneous verse of Blok, treat of such themes as sickness and death. Within the context of the artistic *avant-garde*, however, the stylistic development of the 'Blue Rose' after 1907 is more important. In the 'disillusioned' pictures of Kuznetsov one discerns a certain crystallization of form, a return from the elusive, allusive shapes of the Symbolist works to a more solid presentation of visual reality; at the same time refined graphic delineation is still missing and figures and objects are simplified or vulgarized. In the parallel work of Sapunov and Sudeykin this process is emphasized by their new concern with bright, primitive colours.

These developments represented a new direction which was already affecting other artists in Moscow and the provinces such as D. D. Burlyuk (1882–1967), N. S. Goncharova (1881–1962) and M. F. Larionov (1881–1964): this new direction came to be known as Neo-primitivism. While the formation of Russian Neo-primitivism was stimulated to a certain extent by the models of western artists such as Gauguin, Matisse and Rousseau with which Russian artists were familiar either from trips to Paris or from visits to the private modern art collections of I. A. Morozov (1871–1921) and S. I. Shchukin (1854–1937), it must be stressed that the movement was essentially an indigenous one. In this sense it owed its inspiration not only to the later work of the 'Blue Rose', but also, particularly after 1908, to a renewed interest in primitive, peasant art forms – the *lubok*, shop signboards, icons, wood-carving, children's drawing, etc. The results of this new artistic credo were immediately apparent in the choice of subject-matter – peasants at work, scenes from soldiers' life, still-lives – and in the consciously gross, childish approach to the pictorial surface.

The first Russian Neo-primitivist works were shown at an important series of exhibitions organized between the end of 1907 and the winter of 1910, a period which marked the beginning of the 'boom' in *avant-garde* exhibitions, groups and publications. Among the most impressive of these were the three 'Golden Fleece' shows of 1908, 1909 and 1909/10 at which, except for the third, western artists such as Braque, Matisse and Rouault were also well represented. But perhaps the most sensational exhibitions were those inspired and dominated by D. Burlyuk, later to

Mikhail Larionov, 'Spring' (1912).

Natal'ya Goncharova, 'The Carriers' (1910).

be known as the 'Father of Russian Futurism', namely, the sessions of the 'Wreath-Stephanos' (*Venok-Stefanos*) and the 'Link', at the second of which Burlyuk issued his first loud, anti-social manifesto.[11] But despite Burlyuk's noise and arresting artistic innovations, the real leadership of the Neo-primitivists was, deservedly, claimed by Larionov and Goncharova whose soldier and peasant scenes respectively, such as 'Spring' (1912, Private Collection, Paris) and 'The Carriers' (1910, Private Collection, Paris) provided Russian painting with a fresh, almost barbaric vigour. Although a Neo-primitivist manifesto was published only in 1913, by the painter and colleague of Larionov, A. V. Shevchenko (1882–1948), the movement, as moulded by Larionov and Goncharova, achieved wide recognition in 1910 with the formation of the 'Knave of Diamonds' group.[12] This group, organized by Larionov, held its first exhibition in the winter of 1910/11 in Moscow at which most contributions were executed in the Neo-primitivist style and at which many leftists already famous or about to be so were represented, including David Burlyuk and his brother Vladimir (1886–1917), A. A. Ekster (1884–1949), R. R. Fal'k (1886–1958), Goncharova, P. P. Konchalovsky (1876–1956), A. V. Kuprin (1880–1960), Larionov, A. V. Lentulov (1883–1943), K. S. Malevich (1878–1935), I. I. Mashkov (1881–1944) and A. A. Morgunov (1884–1935), as well as V. V. Kandinsky (1866–1944), Aleksey von Jawlensky (1864–1949) and other representatives of the Munich school. With the foundation of the 'Knave of Diamonds', the movement of Futurism or, as it was called variously in the context of the visual arts, Cubo-futurism, was introduced into the Russian artistic arena, although Russian Futurism as such was established 'officially' only at the end of 1912 with the publication of the Burlyuk/Mayakovsky/Kruchonykh/Khlebnikov proclamation, *A Slap in the Face of Public Taste*. The 'Knave of Diamonds' itself, however, suffered a serious rift late in 1911 when Larionov and Goncharova left it, accusing their colleagues of servility to Paris and neglect of national and eastern artistic sources. The result was that two directions emerged: one, more experimental, led by Larionov and Goncharova; the other, retaining the original

---

[11] D. Burlyuk helped to organize several exhibitions which employed the term 'Wreath', i.e. *Venok-Stefanos*, Moscow, December 1907–January 1908; *Venok-Stefanos*, St Petersburg, March–April 1909, and later in the year in other towns; *Venok*, which opened within the larger exhibition, *Treugol'nik*, St Petersburg, March 1910; in addition, there was an exhibition, *Venok*, which ran in St Petersburg between March and April 1908 but without any contribution from D. Burlyuk. The 'Link' exhibition in Kiev ran during November 1908; D. Burlyuk's manifesto issued at this exhibition was entitled 'Voice of an Impressionist – in Defence of Painting'.

[12] Several artists claimed to have invented the name, Larionov because he liked the combination of letters, Lentulov because the image reminded him of fellow outcasts, i.e. the pattern on a Russian prisoner's uniform.

name although more western, specifically Cubist, led by Konchalovsky and Lentulov. While it is fashionable to emphasize the audacious achievements of the Larionov faction, its counterpart should not be ignored: the post-1911 'Knave of Diamonds' society, which existed as an exhibition society until 1917, made a significant contribution to the evolution of Russian art both in its serious, sometimes pedantic study of painterly problems and in its promotion of such artists as N. I. Al'tman (1889–1970) and Marc Chagall (b. 1887).

Larionov's splinter group won acclaim from three decisive exhibitions which he organized before leaving Moscow in 1914 – the 'Donkey's Tail' (1912), the 'Target' (1913) and 'No. 4' (1914) – the first two of which were the most important since they advanced both new, dynamic personalities and new artistic directions. Although the 'Donkey's Tail'[13] was dominated by the many canvases of Larionov and Goncharova, the contributions of Malevich, Shevchenko and V. Ye. Tatlin (1885–1953) attracted a great deal of attention. For example, Tatlin's concern with the curve and volume brought forth comments on the 'scrolls and semicircles'[14] of his costume designs displayed there and anticipated his first reliefs of the following year. Ostensibly, the exhibition was organized to emphasize the assertion by Larionov and Goncharova that the west had nothing new to offer Russian artists and that artistic inspiration must be sought from primitive art forms of Russia and the east. This idea was made apparent by the predominant choice of peasant/soldier themes both in their work and in that of Malevich and Shevchenko. At the same time the exhibitions advanced the first attempts at what Larionov was going to call Rayonism, exemplified here by such works as 'Snapshot' (present whereabouts unknown) and 'Head of a Soldier' (Leonard Hutton Galleries, New York). Larionov's theory of Rayonism was published in 1913 and advocated in visual terms at the 'Target' exhibition in the spring of that year, although there have been suggestions that Larionov had formulated his basic tenets as early as the spring of 1912.[15] While pictorially the results of Rayonism were exciting in their almost abstract

---

[13] The name was a direct reference to the donkey's tail affair at the Paris Salon des Indépendants in 1909.

[14] From V. Parkin's review in *Oslinyy khvost i mishen'*, Moscow, 1913, p. 52.

[15] The first edition of Larionov's essay on Rayonism, 'Luchistskaya zhivopis'', appeared in *Oslinyy khvost* . . . and, after its conclusion, bore the date June 1912 (even though the miscellany, *Oslinyy khvost* . . ., appeared only in 1913). Despite the many suggestions that Larionov was painting in a Rayonist manner as early as 1911 (even as early as 1909), there is *no* concrete evidence in the form of exhibition catalogues, reviews or contemporaneous articles to support such a view. If we can believe the date of June 1912 above, then it would seem probable that Larionov was thinking in Rayonist terms by the late spring of that year – although even this assumption is not proved by contemporaneous sources.

combinations of colour and line, the written programme was pseudo-scientific and obscure: 'We perceive a sum of rays coming from the source of light which are reflected from the object and fall into our field of vision ... But in order to receive the total sum of rays from the desired object we must wilfully single out only the given object, because together with the rays of the object being perceived there also fall into our field of vision ... rays of other objects.'[16] At the 'Target' Rayonism was illustrated by such works as Larionov's 'Rayonist Sausage and Mackerel' (Private Collection, Paris) and Goncharova's 'Cats' (Guggenheim Museum, New York) and a host of similar titles by the leader and followers of the theory; in addition, Cubo-futurism was represented at the 'Target' by Malevich, including his famous 'Knife-grinder' (1912, Yale University), and by Shevchenko. Similarly, the exhibition 'No. 4' showed examples of Rayonism by Larionov and Goncharova as well as interesting essays in urban Futurism by Ekster and V. V. Kamensky (1884–1961).

Larionov and his disciples were also represented at exhibitions organized by the 'Union of Youth', a large, eclectic society based in St Petersburg which, in addition to staging art exhibitions, arranged lectures and patronized dramatic spectacles. It existed formally from 1910 until 1914 and while it supported Cubo-futurism and Rayonism, it also accommo-

Mikhail Larionov, 'Rayonist Sausage and Mackerel' (1912).

[16] M. Larionov, *Luchizm*, Moscow, 1913, p. 17 (trans. J.B.).

Aleksandr Shevchenko, 'Rayonism' (1913).

dated a highly subjectivist and synthesist kind of painting identifiable by the term Expressionism. It was within the framework of the 'Union of Youth' that Germanic and Russian aspects of Modernism met, since associates of this society, such as the 'crazy doctor', N. I. Kul'bin (1868–1917), were in direct correspondence with *Der blaue Reiter* and later with Walden's *Der Sturm*. In this respect, it is interesting to find that several of the theoretical and practical contributors to the 'Union of Youth' were of Baltic origin, such as the gifted engraver V. N. Masyutin (1884–1955) and the artist and critic V. I. Markov (pseudonym of Waldemars Matvejs, 1877–1914). Indeed, it is within the 'Union of Youth' and, generally, in the northern capital that we encounter the darker, more Teutonic aspects of Modernist Russian painting: above all, we find P. N. Filonov (1883–1941) who, during this early period, was still concerned with the dark mists of Russian legend and pre-history, but who, unlike the Neo-primitivists, was already expressing his fundamental notion that reality was chaos and could be overcome only by a supreme intellectual effort. Al'tman, the Burlyuks, Ye. G. Guro (1877–1913), I. V. Klyun (1870–1942), Malevich and M. V. Matyushin (1861–1934),

Pavel Filonov, 'West and East' (1912–13).

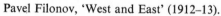

Ivan Klyun, 'Landscape Running Past' (1913).

to mention but a few, were also fellow members of the 'Union of Youth'.

The presence of Malevich at both the 'Knave of Diamonds' and the 'Union of Youth' exhibitions was symptomatic of his growing prestige within the Russian *avant-garde*. It was as early as 1913, in fact, that Malevich had begun to develop an artistic system which in 1915 was to culminate in his formulation of Suprematism; his aspiration towards absolute or self-sufficient art was demonstrated in one of his designs for a backdrop to the Kruchonykh/Matyushin opera, *Victory Over the Sun*, produced under the auspices of the 'Union of Youth' in December 1913 – this was a square divided diagonally into two halves, one white the other black, and framed by an outer square, which, possibly, was a non-

Kazimir Malevich, 'Eight Red Rectangles' (1915).

representational composition. However, although Malevich may have been thinking in terms of abstraction in 1913 and 1914, his canvases submitted to the Larionov exhibitions and to those of the 'Union of Youth' did not present Suprematism, but were thematic exercises in Cubo-futurism. This was true even of the dynamic exhibition 'Tramway V' (Petrograd, spring 1915), subtitled the 'First Futurist Exhibition of Pictures', organized by the *avant-garde* artist I. A. Puni (Pougny) (1894–1956); nevertheless, a sculptural counterpart to Suprematism was presented at the exhibition in the form of Tatlin's painterly reliefs – abstract combinations of metal, glass and wood applied directly to the surface of a board. It was at one of the last extremist exhibitions of the pre-Revolutionary period, '0.10. The Last Futurist Exhibition of Pictures', again organized by Puni in the winter of 1915/16 in Petrograd, that a platform was erected for the formal presentation of Suprematism; accompanied by a Suprematist manifesto signed by Puni, his wife, K. P. Boguslavskaya (1892–1972) *et al.* and by the simultaneous publication of Malevich's book, *From Cubism to Suprematism. The New Painterly Realism*, the first public showing of Suprematist works was given.[17] Although none of Malevich's contributions was called specifically Suprematist, it was clear that such titles as 'Square' (i.e. 'Black Square on White Background', 1915, TG) and 'Painterly Realism of Coloured Masses in Two Dimensions' (1915)[18] were illustrations to the theoretical premise advanced in his book: 'Only when the conscious habit disappears of seeing nature's little nooks, Madonnas and Venuses in pictures, *will we witness a purely painterly work of art* ... I have transformed myself *in the zero of form* and have fished myself out of the *rubbishy slough of Academic art* ... *Objects have vanished like smoke: to attain the new artistic culture*, art advances towards creation as an end in itself and towards domination over the forms of nature ...'[19] Other examples of non-figurative art were provided by Klyun and, on a rather different level, in sculpture by Puni and Tatlin; in addition, Cubo-futurism was well

[17] It is known that Malevich participated in the large exhibition, 'Exhibition of Painting, 1915', in Moscow in 1915, although his name did not appear in the càtalogue. It is remotely possible, therefore, that he contributed Suprematist works to it.
[18] This was the kind of title used by Malevich in the Catalogue to '0.10' (here no. 47), although it is difficult to identify original exhibits with extant canvases because, in many cases, titles have been changed. However, some can be recognized from photographic sources, e.g. compare reproductions on p. 93 of *Malevich*, Stedelijk Museum, Amsterdam, 1970 (compiled by Troels Andersen) with the photograph of '0.10' on p. 81 of H. Berninger and J. Cartier, *Pougny*, Tübingen, 1972.
[19] The book in question saw three editions: *Ot kubizma k suprematizmu. Novyy zhivopisnyy realizm,* Petrograd, 1915; *Ot kubizma k suprematizmu. Novyy zhivopisnyy realizm,* Petrograd, 1916; *Ot kubizma i futurizma k suprematizmu. Novyy zhivopisnyy realizm,* Moscow, 1916. The quotation is from the third edition, p. 2 (trans. J.B.).

Ivan Puni (Jean Pougny), 'Suprematist Sculpture' (1915).

represented by L. S. Popova (1899–1924), O. V. Rozanova (1886–1918) and N. A. Udal'tsova (1886–1961).

The last major pre-Revolutionary leftist exhibition was the 'Shop' organized by Tatlin in Moscow in the spring of 1916. This exhibition was, however, less provocative than the preceding enterprises, since the vast majority of contributions were thematic, Cubo-futurist pictures and, in the case of Malevich, dated from 1913/14. Tatlin, however, submitted seven reliefs, two of them counter-reliefs, and two new, important artists made their appearance – L. A. Bruni (1894–1948) with two tri-planear reliefs and A. M. Rodchenko (1891–1956) with a series of drawings.

The 'Shop' demonstrated that leftist art had lost some of its earlier force and that the age of sensational discoveries and loud declarations in the sphere of easel painting was already passing. The depletion of the artists' ranks and the shortage of basic materials caused by the First World War tended to enforce the general feeling that Russian art had entered a state of crisis, even an impasse. It was the Revolution which both verified this situation and suggested a tentative answer to the artist's predicament.

Architecture

As in the case of Russian painting, the 1850s marked a period of transition in the development of Russian architecture. By the closing years of that decade the simplicity and rationality of the neo-Classical movement in architecture had been lost to eclecticism and increased decorativism. At the same time a rapid advancement in building began to take place, especially in the urban centres because of new industrialization and railway expansion. Factories, railway stations and workers' settlements (often complexes of mere wooden shacks) therefore constituted the basic types of construction in the 1860s and 1870s. The 1860s witnessed a distinct architectural decline as aristocratic taste gave way to the mercantile prerequisites of cheapness and efficiency, and the result was both the loss of a definitive architectural style and the emergence of extremely pernicious elements in building as a whole. Little attention was paid to local environment (e.g. workers' dwellings were constructed on factory premises), landscape planning was quite neglected (often the architectural unity of ancient towns was ruined by the sudden appearance of railway stations in their midst) and essential facilities such as damp courses and drainage were often ignored.

By the early 1870s, however, a few enlightened architects attempted to revive specific styles of the past, notably the Byzantine and pre-Petrine Russian styles. Although by the mid-1870s the cult of Byzantium was recognized officially and enjoyed fashionable popularity, its application was confined almost exclusively to new church architecture and scarcely affected other types of building. Of more importance during the 1870s and the ensuing decades was the Neo-nationalist or Neo-Russian style, which was incorporated into all types of buildings, private and public, wooden and stone. The initial champions of Neo-nationalism were V. A. Gartman (1834–73) and I. P. Ropet (pseudonym of I. N. Petrov, 1845–1908) whose energies produced two of the most memorable Neo-nationalist buildings, both at Abramtsevo: the workshop/studio (by Gartman, 1873) and the bath-house (by Ropet, 1874). It was significant, of course, that Abramtsevo should have provided an outlet for their artistic talents, for it was here, too, that painters and sculptors were turning their attention to pre-Petrine peasant art and architecture, applying stylized, ancient, peasant motifs to their own works. One must therefore regard the Neo-nationalist tendency in architecture not as an isolated phenomenon, but as an integral part of the whole Neo-nationalist movement which affected literature, music and painting in the 1870s.

The strength of the new architectural style, nicknamed derisively *ropetovshchina* by its antagonists, increased significantly as a result of its popularization by the influential journal *Architect* (*Zodchiy*, founded 1872), and it was not long before important city buildings were affected. It was natural that as a more indigenous and traditional centre, Moscow and not St Petersburg should have been the first testing-ground for the new style, and by the mid-1870s several large-scale, Neo-nationalist

Moscow, Verkhniye Torgovyye Ryady (now GUM) (A. N. Pomerantsev, 1889–93).

St Petersburg, Church of the Resurrection (A. A. Parland, 1882–1907).

buildings had been constructed there, e.g. the Polytechnical Museum (I. A. Monigetti and N. A. Shokhin, 1875–7) and the restaurant 'Slavonic Bazaar' (A. L. Gun and P. N. Kudryavtsev, 1873). As with artistic designs produced at Abramtsevo, Neo-nationalist architects tended to borrow traditional motifs from such diverse sources as embroidery, tray decoration, icon-painting and wood-carving and to apply them indiscriminately to a totally different surface. Consequently, however decorative and novel façades and porticoes suddenly became – with fire-birds on coloured glazed tiles or fretted, stone window-frames – the result seemed often capricious and eclectic. One observer, speaking in 1881, summed up the situation by identifying the salient features of contemporary architecture as 'marble hand-woven towels and brick embroideries'. Throughout the rest of the nineteenth century and during the early twentieth Neo-nationalism left its mark on many buildings, and one has merely to stand in the vicinity of Red Square to see such impressive examples as the Historical Museum (A. A. Semyonov and V. O. Sherwood, 1873–83), GUM stores (A. N. Pomerantsev, 1889–93) and the adjacent Lenin Museum (formerly the Moscow Duma, D. N. Chichagov, 1890–2). In addition, the style affected numerous blocks of apartments especially during the 1880s and 1890s and was assimilated readily by church architecture – of which the Church of the Resurrection in St Petersburg (the so-called *na krovi*) is probably the most important example (A. A. Parland, 1882–1907).

Despite the neglect of landscape planning and poor quality construction which followed in the wake of the industrial boom of the 1860s, certain positive contributions were made by industry to the evolution of Russian architecture. Automatically, industry acquainted architects with 'modern' materials such as cast iron and glass, a development which was paralleled by an upsurge of interest in modern western buildings such as covered markets, hot-houses, railway stations and, of course, the Crystal Palace which, for several years, had already been employing iron and glass on a substantial scale. One of the most successful examples of engineering applied to architecture during this period was the covered market in St Petersburg designed by I. S. Kitner *et al.* in 1883: with its iron framework, glass roof and large covered space, it incorporated very positive western innovations and formed the prototype of several such Russian markets. Above all, of course, this bold conception of architecture manifested itself in the construction of railway stations, although the first attempts in this field were mere variations on conventional designs for large public halls. After the completion of the Odessa Station (V. A. Shreter, 1879–83), however, with its spacious interior and glass roof, the golden age of Russian railway architecture was ushered in; and although many subsequent stations sported elaborate Neo-nationalist façades such as the Moscow Yaroslavl' Station (F. O. Shekhtel', 1903–4) and the Kazan' Station (A. V. Shchusev, 1913–26), they retained that utilitarianism and spaciousness which we associate with the great American and European stations. The attention to iron framework and glass roofing encountered in railway stations was indicative of the general application of such principles to many types of buildings at that time, especially the so-called *passazhi* or two/three storey complexes of shops of which GUM on Red Square provides a good example. Banks, stock exchanges and even museums – e.g. the Pushkin Museum of Fine Arts in Moscow (R. I. Klein, 1898–1912) where the glass roofing was particularly appropriate – bowed to the aesthetics of glass and iron. The new concern with function, rather than with decoration, gave rise in turn to more rational projects for hospitals, schools and apartment houses in which specific consideration was given to drainage, natural lighting and anti-fire precautions (see, for example, the Leningrad Institute of Midwifery and Gynaecology, L. N. Benois, 1898–1904).

Gradually the uncontrolled, sporadic building development which had been the fruit of industrial expansion after 1860 came to be replaced by the more disciplined, more scientific attitude of town planning and the problems of pollution, sanitation and the preservation of historic monuments began to receive greater attention. The Siberian town of Dal'niy (now part of Chinese territory) built as an ice-free port at the terminus of the Eastern Chinese Railway (K. G. Slonimsky *et al.*, 1899–1904) afforded a convincing example of this new urban policy: its complex of streets founded on the rational, French Baroque principle, its landscaped park areas and balanced distribution of public buildings were concepts which anticipated the dynamic projects of the great urban planners of the 1920s.

Moscow, Yaroslavl' Station (F. O. Shekhtel', 1903–4).

Despite the move towards rationality, the late nineteenth and early twentieth centuries were still very much a period of eclecticism, witness to which was the simultaneous manipulation of many diverse styles. In Moscow alone, for example, striking visual contrast was achieved between the Chinese Tea Shop on Myasnitskaya (now Kirov Street, R. I. Klein, 1893), the Myur and Meriliz store (now the TsUM stores, Klein, late 1900s) and the Kiev Station (I. I. Rerberg, 1912–17). Nevertheless, one distinctive, original style did emerge in the 1890s: this was Art Nouveau or *style moderne* which owed its formation in Russia both to western influence and to the stylization of Neo-nationalism. The curved lines and elongated plant decoration which we associate with Art Nouveau appeared in much of the contemporaneous work of F. O. Shekhtel' (1859–1926), particularly in his designs for the houses of I. V. Morozov (1895) and S. T. Mamontov (1897) and the famous villa of S. P. Ryabushinsky (1900–2, now the Gor'ky Museum), all in Moscow. One factor especially identifiable with Art Nouveau architecture in Russia – and which was practised, above all, in Moscow – was the incorporation of monumental painting into façades executed in mosaics or glazed tiles, e.g. Vrubel''s frieze for the Hotel Metropol' (W. Walcott *et al.*, 1899–1909). The application of external decoration to buildings by such painters as K. Korovin, Rerikh and Vrubel' was probably one of the most significant contributions which Art Nouveau gave to contemporaneous Russian architecture, and examples on both official and

Moscow, Myur and Meriliz store (now TsUM) (R. I. Klein, late 1900s).

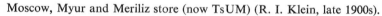

142

apartment buildings in Moscow and St Petersburg are very common. This tendency can be explained by the general move at this time towards artistic synthesism and, more specifically, by the decorative conventions which Neo-nationalism had already established. In this context it is relevant to draw attention to the folklore ornaments on the Dom Pertsova (Kursovoy Pereulok, Moscow, S. V. Malyutin, 1905–7) and the central part of the Tret'yakov Gallery (V. M. Vasnetsov, 1900–5).

Despite the swirling lines encountered both in the outward appearance of Art Nouveau buildings and in their interiors – staircases, doorways,

Moscow, Villa of Stepan Ryabushinsky (now the Gor'ky Museum) (F. O. Shekhtel', 1900–2).

electroliers, etc. – the sense of rationality gained from industrial experience was not lost. Indeed, parallel to such projects as Ryabushinsky's villa, there was an obvious concern with linearity and spatial control, a fact which aligns many buildings of the 1900s with the Constructivist designs of the 1920s: it is a short step, for example, from the severe lines of the House of the Guards' Economic Society (now the House of Leningrad Trade, N. V. Vasil'yev *et al.*, 1908–9) to the revolutionary projects of the Vesnin brothers or M. Ya. Ginzburg (1892–1946). Similarly, new materials were being tested such as the ferro-concrete in the structure of the Myur and Meriliz Store (TsUM) or the undisguised iron pillars and ferro-concrete walls of A. K. Montag's covered market in St Petersburg (1906). It was as a result of this development that neo-Classicism asserted itself again, its symmetry and purity of form appealing to architects tired of the excesses of Art Nouveau, and many important city buildings realized after 1910 reflect this trend, e.g. Moscow Popular University (now School for the Party Central Committee, I. A. Ivanov-Shits, 1910–13). Shortly before 1917, in fact, a whole generation of neo-Classical architects emerged and produced a series of retrospective villas, apartment blocks and public buildings which anticipated the Palladian revival under Stalin: and it was such neo-Classicists as I. A. Fomin (1872–1936), A. V. Shchusev (1873–1949) and I. V. Zholtovsky (1867–1959) who were to maintain their traditionalist principles and attain such popularity under Stalin's inflexible regime.

4

ART AND ARCHITECTURE IN
SOVIET RUSSIA, 1917-1972

Art

The years immediately following the October Revolution are observed conventionally by art historians as a period of struggle between cultural extremes which ended in the early 1930s with the liquidation, albeit apparent, of 'formalism' and the triumph of the school of Socialist Realism. Essentially, this is so – leftist trends in painting and sculpture were being condemned officially well before 1930 – but the emergent discipline of Socialist or, as it was often called before 1932, Heroic Realism should not be censured immediately because of this. Ostensibly, the advocation of Realist principles was a return to the tendentious art of the second half of the nineteenth century, but this was, in fact, an interpretation which achieved results considerably different from those of the Wanderers. It is necessary, therefore, to approach the whole of post-1917 Russian art not with the attitude that it 'stopped' with the 1932 Decree, 'On the Reconstruction of Literary and Art Organizations', but rather that it has given us a new pictorial dimension and has provided a tentative answer to our own artistic fragmentation.

Immediately after 1917 most artistic groupings were destroyed or at least temporarily disbanded. Progressive artists, once persecuted by critics and public alike, suddenly found themselves accepted as the heralds of the Revolution, since it was argued that the broken forms of their Cubo-futurism, Suprematism, etc. had mirrored unconsciously the impending disintegration of a whole society.[1] No longer was there the need to 'shock the bourgeoisie' with such striking names as the 'Knave of Diamonds' or 'Tramway V', no longer the need to retreat into the exclusive protection of groups. Responsible for the artist's improved position were the innovations of Narkompros (People's Commissariat for Enlightenment) organized in November 1917 under the auspices of A. V. Lunacharsky (1875–

---

[1] See, for example, statements by K. Malevich in his *O novykh sistemakh v iskusstve*, Vitebsk, 1919, p. 10 and El Lissitzky in his 'New Russian Art', in *El Lissitzky: Life, Letters, Texts* by S. Lissitsky-Küppers, London, 1968, p. 331.

1933). Although the latter was certainly lenient towards leftist art, the initial policies of Narkompros on the visual arts were formulated to a great extent by the Head of the Visual Arts Department (IZO) within Narkompros, D. V. Shterenberg (1881–1948), together with his many radical colleagues – including Al'tman, Malevich, N. N. Punin (1888–1953) and Tatlin. It was thanks to this collective of far-sighted artists and theorists that State commissions were placed with the *avant-garde*, that their works were bought for museums, that exhibitions of *avant-garde* art were sponsored officially and, above all, that such momentous projects as the universal reorganization of art education and the establishment of the Institute of Artistic Culture (Inkhuk) were realized. Inevitably, such a beneficial situation was of short duration and, ultimately, government assistance changed into government dictatorship: we find, for example, that as early as 1920 representationalism was being favoured in political circles, while other trends were being criticized.[2]

The most dynamic centres of artistic activity after 1917 were the new art schools organized by Narkompros. In 1918 under the auspices of Tatlin in Moscow and Shterenberg in Petrograd, the Moscow Institute of Painting, Sculpture and Architecture and the Stroganov Art School were integrated to form the Free State Art Studios (Svomas – later Vkhutemas/Vkhutein),[3] and the St Petersburg Academy was abolished to be replaced by the Petrograd State Free Art Educational Studios (Pegoskhuma – later Svomas and then the Academy again).[4] Moscow maintained its traditional status as the focus of *avant-garde* strength and Vkhutemas became the pivot of the bitter conflict between the artistic left and right. Many of the pre-Revolutionary leftists such as Malevich, Popova and Rodchenko became professors there and opened departments founded on their theories; at the same time more conservative artists such as V. A. Favorsky (1886–1964) and V. I. Shukhayev (1887–1973) also held teaching posts, so that students were able to choose from a whole range of diverse courses. A similar pattern of reconstruction was evident in the provinces where audacious innovations were made in methods of instruction and in actual creative output: the famous lithographic studio of L. M. (El) Lissitzky (1890–1941) at Vitebsk and the authority of Chagall there (replaced by Malevich at the end of 1919) made it one of the most innovative art centres outside Moscow.

A dominant force in Russian *avant-garde* developments after 1917 was Inkhuk, organized in Moscow in May 1920, and its later affiliations in

---

[2] See, for example, 'Open Letter from the Central Committee', in *Pravda*, 1 December 1920.

[3] Renamed Vkhutemas (Higher State Art-Technical Studios) in 1920 and Vkhutein (Higher State Art-Technical Institute) in 1926; in 1930 changed to the Moscow Art Institute.

[4] Renamed Svomas in 1919 and then changed back to the Academy in 1921.

Petrograd and Vitebsk. Most of the leftist artists were attached to Inkhuk and key positions were occupied variously by Kandinsky (in Moscow), Tatlin (in Petrograd) and Malevich (in Vitebsk). One of the main functions of Inkhuk was to reduce the principal modern movements such as Suprematism and the 'culture of materials' to a scientifically based programme which could be used for educational and research purposes – a development somewhat akin to the first endeavours of the Russian literary Formalists. The contribution of Inkhuk to artistic thinking was twofold, for it was there that both the so-called 'laboratory art' and 'productional art' were developed. The former, advocated by Kandinsky, came to be rejected by the majority of the Inkhuk members as too aesthetic and irrelevant to the needs of a technological society. As a result Kandinsky left Inkhuk and in the summer of 1921 entered the commission for the establishment of the Academy of Artistic Sciences where he presented a version of his Inkhuk programme; subsequently, Kandinsky incorporated some of his original ideas into his teaching methods at the Bauhaus. The productional art group was undoubtedly the more influential of the factions within Inkhuk and contributed substantially to the rise of Constructivism in the autumn of 1921: the concern with concrete material, with the 'object' (*veshch'*), shared by productional art supporters such as the Stenberg brothers, Georgy (1900–33) and Vladimir (b. 1899), and the numerous publications of its brilliant apologists such as B. I. Arvatov (1896–1940), O. M. Brik (1888–1945), B. A. Kushner (1888–1937) and N. M. Tarabukin (1899–1956) were bound to affect the evolution of Soviet art.[5]

El Lissitzky, 'Proun Construction 1A' (1919).

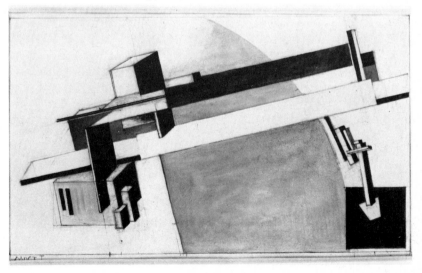

[5] For details concerning Inkhuk, including Kandinsky's programme, see I. Matsa *et al.*,

The very diversity of courses at Vkhutemas and the conflicts within Inkhuk were symptomatic of the general mood of indecision which, even before the Revolution, had confronted easel painting and sculpture. In 1915 Malevich had formulated Suprematism, the absolute in art, and this had controverted immediately the function of art as a reflection of reality, replacing it by the work as an end in itself. Whether the philosophy of this 'new painterly realism' was a reprocessing of the theory of 'art for art's sake' or whether it was a genuine reappraisal of the artistic situation was a question immaterial to a new society eager to advance on all fronts towards a utilitarian, material culture. Leading artists were quick to realize that abstract combinations of colours or linear rhythms were of little use to the new clientèle, the mass, and that art had to be given a new direction or revert to a more intelligible, accessible theoretical foundation. Alternatively, as members of the Proletkul′t organization (established formally in February 1917) hastened to affirm, art had to be directly relevant to the proletariat and, consequently, should develop primarily within an industrial framework – leading to emphasis on applied art and productional design. The attitude of the masses towards abstract and semi-abstract art was well demonstrated in their violent reaction to some of the more provocative statues erected in Moscow in 1918 and after in connexion with Lenin's plan of monumental propaganda:[6] some of the Cubo-futurist contributions were met with angry protests and the figure of Bakunin modelled by B. D. Korolyov (1885–1963) was eventually dismantled because of the protests against its schematic, twisted forms.

The realization that art in its present state had reached an impasse contributed directly to the birth of Constructivism. The prelude to this was the exhibition '5 × 5 = 25', organized by Rodchenko in September 1921 in Moscow, at which the works and personal manifestos of the artists – Ekster, Popova, Rodchenko, Stepanova and A. A. Vesnin (1883–1959) – were epitomized by the three canvases of Rodchenko painted respectively red, yellow and blue (a minimalist treatment which Rodchenko also applied to his free-standing and suspended constructions of 1918–21). It was shortly after this showing, in November of the same year, that the five participants together with their colleagues made a joint declaration

Sovetskoye iskusstvo za 15 let, Moscow–Leningrad, 1933, pp. 126–42; for details concerning the Academy of Artistic Sciences, including Kandinsky's programme, see *Iskusstvo* (Zhurnal Rossiyskoy akademii khudozhestvennykh nauk), Moscow, 1923, no. 1, pp. 407–49.
[6] Lenin's plan, issued as the Decree, 'On the Demolition of Monuments Erected in Honour of the Tsars and their Servants and the Formulation of Projects of Monuments to the Russian Socialist Revolution', was issued in April 1918. Details of the plan can be found in M. Neiman, 'Leninskiy plan "Monumental′noy propagandy" i pervyye skul′pturnyye pamyatniki' in *Istoriya russkogo iskusstva* (ed. I. Grabar′ *et al.*), vol. XI, Moscow, 1957, pp. 23–53.

at Inkhuk to the effect that they acknowledged 'self-sufficient easel painting as extinct and our activity as mere painters useless' and advocated the 'absoluteness of productional art and Constructivism as its only form of expression'.[7] This decision culminated in their rejection of easel painting and their direct orientation towards industrial design – textiles, typography, cinematography. For other artists such as Naum Gabo (1890–1978), Antoine Pevsner (1886–1962), K. K. Medunetsky (b. 1899) and, initially, Tatlin, Constructivism was something outside applied art or artistic design, a product of the inherent qualities of material itself, as

Lyubov′ Popova, 'Painterly Architectonics' (*c.* 1918).

[7] Quoted from V. Lobanov, *Khudozhestvennyye gruppirovki za 25 let* (Moscow, 1930), p. 101.

the celebrated 'Realistic Manifesto' of 1920 proclaimed so forcefully. Tatlin's Tower, projected as a monument to the Third International, well demonstrated such a doctrine, for in spite of its various utilitarian functions (*it* was intended as a conference centre and a telegraph office, among other things) it would have remained an aesthetic, independent creation in metal. Although planned early in 1919, before Constructivism emerged as a formal movement, Tatlin's Tower serves perhaps as the most striking example of 'Labour, technology, organization!'[8] It was not long, however, before the purity of this school of Constructivism was lost to the more eclectic principles of applied art, so that by 1925 Constructivism had become a blanket term for any angular designs applied to furniture, fabrics, porcelain or theatre sets, and only in the sphere of architecture were its original rationality and economy preserved until about 1930.

Aleksandr Rodchenko, 'Construction' (1921).

[8] A. Gan, *Konstruktivizm*, Tver', 1922, p. 48.

The profound effect of the new concept of art on theatre décor, book illustration, poster and street decoration deserves a separate monograph. Suffice it to say that industrial Constructivism served to accelerate a movement which had been well in evidence before 1921: for example, Cubo-futurist designs by Al'tman, Kuprin, Shterenberg and others had been applied to the large-scale mass decorations in 1918 in honour of the first anniversary of the October Revolution, and 'agit' motifs can be discerned in many studio works of the same period. Indeed, the intense concern with design was part of an indigenous tradition which was traceable at least to the stylization and simplicity of much 'World of Art' work – by Bakst, Benois, Somov, etc.; and it was a tradition not completely annulled by the repressive measures of the early 1930s, for book illustration and theatre décor, in particular, remained as oases for the more imaginative, more flexible artistic mind.

Although 1922 marked the flowering of the Constructivist movement in art, a tendency diametrically opposed in aims and output came to the fore at what is regarded as the first exhibition of the famous Association of Artists of Revolutionary Russia (AKhRR) in May of that year.[9] The

Kazimir Medunetsky, 'Construction no. 557' (1919).

Aleksandra Ekster, costume design for Tairov's production of *Romeo and Juliet* at the Kamernyy Theatre, Moscow (1921).

[9] The exhibition was called 'Exhibition of Pictures by Artists of the Realist Direction' and opened in Moscow on 1 May 1922; AKhRR was established immediately thereafter. AKhRR changed its name to AKhR (Association of Artists of the Revolution) in 1928; it was dissolved by the 1932 Decree.

inspiration of this group was derived from the Wanderers society, resurrected in the spring of 1922. Their traditions of a socially tendentious Realism were reformulated in the decisive declaration of AKhRR signed by painters both of the older generation such as Malyutin and of the younger such as Ye. A. Katsman (1890–1976): 'The Great October Revolution, in liberating the creative forces of the people, has aroused the consciousness of the masses and the artists – the spokesmen of the people's spiritual life . . . We will provide a true picture of events and not abstract concoctions discrediting our Revolution in the face of the international proletariat . . . and now we must reveal our artistic experiences in the monumental forms of the style of Heroic Realism.'[10] This and the ensuing declarations of AKhRR laid the foundation of a direction which was subsequently to be called Socialist Realism.

Of course, the important developments of 1921 and 1922 by no means halted the activities of leftist easel painters, even though their position was threatened by the move towards industry on the one hand and towards Realism on the other. The grand exhibition of Russian art, organized by IZO Narkompros and held in the Van Diemen Gallery, Berlin in 1922 demonstrated, despite the large number of earlier works, that painting and sculpture could still be treated as progressive art forms. The contributions of such diverse leftists as Al'tman, A. D. Drevin (1889–1938), Filonov, Gabo, P. A. Mansurov (b. 1896) and Shterenberg proved that easel art was obliged to surrender neither its independence to applied art, nor its flexibility to a single ideology – at least not yet.

Natan Al'tman, 'Petrokommuna'   Aleksandr Drevin, 'Abstraction'
            (1919).   (1921).

[10] Quoted from I. Matsa, op. cit., p. 345 (trans. J.B.).

Despite the renewal of representationalist principles within the ranks of AKhRR a purely photographic naturalism did not emerge, and, indeed, was never advocated. Even in the pictures of I. I. Brodsky (1884–1939) and B. V. Ioganson (1893–1973), painters who often consulted photographic archives, the scenes of revolution or portraits of Lenin contained a crude vitality achieved as much by formal arrangement and colour composition as by photographic likeness. Some of the younger generation of new representationalists such as A. A. Deineka (1899–1969), Yu. I. Pimenov (1903–77), A. G. Tyshler (b. 1898) and P. V. Vil'yams (1902–47), while depicting scenes from everyday life, tended towards a schematic, often highly subjective presentation – clearly identifiable with Deineka's 'Defence of Petrograd' (1927, Central Museum of the Soviet Army, Moscow; artist's copy of 1966 in TG) and Tyshler's 'Woman and an Aeroplane' (1926, Private Collection, Moscow), pictures which evoke such terms as Expressionist and Surrealist; older painters such as N. A. Kasatkin (1859–1930) also attempted to approach their subjects of oppressed workers and scenes from the revolutions and the Civil War aesthetically as well as tendentiously. But whatever their interpretations of reality, the new Soviet painters observed more frequently the principle

Aleksandr Deineka, 'Defence of Petrograd' (1927).

153

Gustav Klutsis, illustration to V. Mayakovsky's poem 'Vladimir Il'ich Lenin' (1925).

of intelligibility and their vivid elucidations of familiar subjects at once made them popular. Indeed, the mid-1920s witnessed the rise of the so-called 'monumental painting' – large panoramas (and later dioramas) of battle scenes, life-sized portraits, extensive mosaics and frescoes – in many ways a revitalization of the traditions of church fresco and iconostasis painting. Such emotive canvases as 'Gun-carriage' (1925, TG) by M. V. Grekov (1882–1934) and Brodsky's 'Shooting of the 26 Baku Commissars' (1925, Museum of the History of the Azerbaijan Party Organization, Baku) revived an important school of Russian battle-painting which produced its finest works during the Second World War. This, together with the rebirth of other genres – the portrait, the landscape and the *intérieur* or domestic scene, formed the mainstream of official Soviet painting which, hitherto, has remained ostensibly unchanged.

Despite the gradual assertion of representationalist and Realist principles in the mid- and late 1920s, the general front of the visual arts was still a very broken one. AKhRR dominated, but it by no means contained all the leading painters of the day and it competed with a whole complex of leftist and more moderate groups. Such organizations as '4 Arts' (exhibiting 1925–8), which proclaimed that 'the content of our works is characterized not by its subjects . . . the subject is merely a pretext for the creative transformation of material into artistic form',[11] the 'Society of Easel Artists' (OST, exhibiting 1925–8) and 'October' (active 1928–32) with its emphasis on the applied and photographic arts presented a serious barrier to the formation of a cohesive Realist discipline. The official inclination towards Realism became increasingly evident as the new palaces of culture came to be furnished with pictures of Revolutionary heroes or industrial landscapes, as museum acquisition of deviationist works ceased and as non-Realist exhibitions were discouraged more and more. The culmination of this political intrusion into art was the Decree issued by the Central Committee of the Party on 23 April 1932, 'On the Reconstruction of Literary and Art Organizations': the government affirmed that existing organizations were too narrow for the new proletarian artists and that some of them were alien to the demands of political and social reality; the remedy was seen to lie in the liquidation of all groups and in the establishment of a general Union of Artists, although the latter was not founded until 1957. Two years after the publication of this Decree Socialist Realism was formally advocated at the First All-Union Writers' Congress and so established the direction that Soviet art and literature were to follow for at least the next twenty years.

The Soviet visual arts of the 1930s were profoundly affected by the move towards Socialist Realism. Although no exhaustive theoretical foundation was ever given to this concept, its basic premise might well be interpreted

[11] Quoted from I. Matsa *et al.*, *Yezhegodnik literatury i iskusstva*, Moscow, 1929, p. 551.

as the depiction of contemporary reality in its revolutionary state and in its optimistic aspiration towards an ideal future – a premise, incidentally, that imbued some of the early Socialist Realist paintings with a curiously Romantic quality. It should be remembered here that the Realist tradition in Russia had not died and, whether in a didactic or in a more sentimental variant, had lived on in the works of artists such as Arkhipov and S. Yu. Zhukovsky (1873–1944). Limitations of space do not allow us to discuss in detail the reasons why a Realist or, at least, Naturalist conception of art was, and is, so popular in Russia, although, by its very nature, Russian art had always been more concerned with 'ethics' than with 'aesthetics' (the icon is an obvious illustration of this). Even in key manifestations of the *avant-garde*, for example in the work of Kandinsky and Malevich, art was linked closely to the 'extra-pictorial' world, i.e. to a philosophical, if not to a narrative, dimension. As recent research has shown, the 'hidden images' in Kandinsky's so-called abstract work were just as representational as the domestic scenes of the 'Wanderers'.

During the 1920s, this powerful tradition of artistic 'relevance' reasserted itself, and the first graduates of the restructured art schools such as Deineka, Goncharov and Pimenov immediately favoured an art form that was topical. As indicated above, their preference was for an interpretation of Expressionism (especially in the case of Pimenov) and, like the later German Expressionists (Georg Grosz and Otto Dix), they used an austere and graphic form to render subjects of socio-political importance – the NEP bourgeoisie, the horrors of war and starvation, etc. On this level, the OST artists shared the same principles as the first industrial Constructivists who, in 1921, had rejected abstract art in order to seek their own kind of *art engagé* – in their case, industrial design. Among other Soviet artists who quickly adjusted to the need for social commitment in the 1920s were former members of the more 'western' faction of the 'Knave of Diamonds', especially Konchalovsky, Kuprin and Lentulov. Both before and after the Revolution they had experimented with Cubism, and Lentulov had actually produced a few non-figurative works around 1916, but, essentially, they depicted the concrete world, the 'beautiful flesh of things' as Yakov Tugendkhol'd once said in 1914. In the mid-1920s, many of the former 'Knave of Diamonds' artists joined AKhRR and produced examples of 'heroic realism' such as *Novgorod. Fish Market* (Konchalovsky, 1928) and *Novorossiysk Cement Factory. Interior* (Lentulov, 1929): in terms of colour combination, texture, even pictorial structure, there was sometimes little difference between the pre- and post-Revolutionary work of the 'Knave of Diamonds' artists.

At the risk of inviting immediate censure, one might assert that the disappearance of abstract art from Russia's cultural horizon and the emergence of a new realism were, in many respects, the result of an organic process, a natural reaction which began in the early 1920s, if not before. Of course, there are serious arguments that can be – and should be – advanced against Socialist Realism, but western observers (and, increasingly, Soviet scholars) tend to address their arguments more to the political methods whereby the artistic idea of Socialist Realism was (and is) implemented than to the artistic idea itself. In some ways, the aesthetical theses of Socialist Realism were even innovative and they did provide a degree of direction and of cohesion to the large number of trends and factions still operative in the late 1920s. The fundamental advocacy of a figurative and assertive art form should not bar Socialist Realist art from serious critical appreciation. Nor should its reliance on official patronage: in this respect Socialist Realism had many worthy precedents – from the services of the Old Masters to ecclesiastical power to the willing concentration of the eighteenth-century English portraitists on the upper classes. But during the Stalin era it was the *exclusive* rights of Socialist Realism and the complete denial of cultural plurality that gave Soviet art its negative connotation, rather than the artistic ideals of Socialist Realism itself. The pernicious effects of this political imposition – the untold human suffering, the duplicity and depravity of power – can scarcely be exaggerated, but (if this is possible) their spectre should not be allowed to cast too dark a shadow on the aesthetic ideals of Socialist Realism itself.

Obviously, under the harsh political conditions of Socialist Realism, the tradition of the *avant-garde* was disrupted or, at least, transformed out of all recognition (although very few artists, unlike their literary colleagues, were actually arrested and imprisoned). Some courageous individuals continued to experiment, but, deprived of the opportunity of exhibiting, of an open art market and of sympathetic criticism, they could not disseminate their ideas in any extensive manner. Filonov, for example, was not permitted to exhibit his work between 1934 and 1941 because of his 'alienation' from Realism. This is not to say that the former members of Russia's *avant-garde* ceased their creativity in the 1930s, even though their ranks, by then, were depleted either by emigration (Gabo, Kandinsky, etc.) or by death (Popova, Matyushin, Malevich, etc.). For example, Lissitzky and Rodchenko produced exciting photo-montage work for the propaganda magazine *USSR in Construction*, and in the early 1940s Rodchenko actually began to paint 'Abstract Expressionism' well in advance of Jackson Pollock. During the 1930s Tatlin also returned to painting, with very interesting results. Other artists, such as Shterenberg, sometimes transferred their talents to book or stage design, disciplines that provided rather more artistic license than the studio arts. On the other hand, those artists who had never been a part of the *avant-garde* and who had already begun to portray the new Soviet reality well before 1932 intensified their efforts during the pre-war years: painters such as M. I. Avilov (1882–1954), Ioganson and P. P. Sokolov-Skalya (1899–1961) produced some of their most popular work – pictorial journalese that had, and still has, great appeal to the average Soviet citizen.

Essentially, Socialist Realism was practised during the 1930s in four particular areas of painting – the domestic and intimate genre, portraiture, the industrial and urban landscape, and the collective farm scene. Some of the most powerful pictures of the 1930s enter the first category: Ioganson's 'Interrogation of the Communists' (1933, TG), for example, successfully demonstrates the courage of the oppressed in the face of hardship and, moreover, is technically good. Such themes, however banal, were accepted with alacrity both by the Party and by the masses, and the enthusiasm and optimism germane to such works were incorporated further into the scenes of the Civil War to which such artists as Avilov and G. M. Shegal (1889–1956) returned during this period. Yet despite the popularity of these pictures they were not *contemporary* and did not depict actual Soviet reality in its revolutionary state: this need was answered by the significant output of portraits and landscapes during this decade. Apart from P. D. Korin (1892–1967) few of the younger artists were successful in portrait painting, whereas the older generation

Aleksandr Gerasimov, 'Stalin and Voroshilov in the Kremlin Grounds' (1938).

was particularly fertile. Stalin and government officials formed a favourite subject but interesting pictorial records were made also of members of the professions, e.g. the scientist Pavlov (1935, TG) by M. V. Nesterov (1862–1942), Meyerhold by Konchalovsky (1938, TG), Gor'ky by Brodsky (1937, TG) and the pianist Igumnov by Sar'yan (1934, State Picture Gallery of Armenia, Yerevan). However, similar presentations of ordinary men and women – factory workers and farm workers – were not attempted on any substantial scale and it was not until after the war that this kind of portrait began to receive serious attention. Perhaps the most original developments in Socialist Realist art in the 1930s were the many depictions of industrial and urban complexes. The younger generation proved to be more productive in this field and maintained energetically the traditions

Pyotr Konchalovsky, 'Portrait of Meyerhold' (1938).

already founded in the 1920s by V. N. Yakovlev (1893–1953) and V. V. Meshkov (1893–1963). Such vivid pictures as 'On the Track' (1933, TG) by G. G. Nissky (b. 1903) and 'Higher and Higher' (1934, Kiev Museum of Russian Art) by S. V. Ryangina (1891–1955) showed a dynamic society in the course of constructing an industrial, technological future. The same positive interpretation of socialism was manifest in the scenes from collective farm life by S. A. Chuykov (b. 1902), S. V. Gerasimov (1885–1964) and A. A. Plastov (1893–1972).

The Second World War caused the immediate ideological mobilization of the leading Soviet artists. Painters were sent to the front not only to depict actual events – as many western European artists had done in the First World War – but also to obtain material for large-scale landscapes and portraits, many of which were completed after the war. The early 1940s witnessed, above all, the development of the so-called thematic picture – accounts of real incidents and not generalized, symbolic interpretations. At the same time, affected by the upsurge of patriotism, artists turned to historic moments of Russia's past so that 1942, for example, saw the creation of Korin's triptych, 'Alexander Nevsky' (TG) and of Lansere's military series centred on 1812 (TG). Artists who had been content to describe peaceful landscapes or domestic scenes were now expected to invest their canvases with specifically military or nationalistic features: Plastov, for example, moved from his depictions of rural pleasures to more tendentious pictures such as 'A Fascist Flew Past' (1942, TG) and, similarly, S. Gerasimov gave his outdoor scenes more contemporary meaning as in his 'Mother of a Partisan' (1943, TG). Of particular interest were the war canvases of Deineka: technically well executed, but not merely photographic, such pictures as 'The Defence of Sevastopol'' (1942, RM) and 'Outskirts of Moscow. November' (1941, TG) provided an emotive and artistic commentary on the privations of war. Pimenov and V. A. Serov (1910–69) also produced depictions of true events such as 'Meeting on the Neva. Breach of the Blockade' (1943, RM, by Serov and others), a moment which Serov witnessed personally. Apart from their numerous anti-German caricatures and cartoons, the famous Kukryniksy (the abbreviated name of the closely knit trio, M. V. Kupriyanov (b. 1903), P. N. Krylov (b. 1902) and N. A. Sokolov (b. 1903)) also directed their energies into topical easel paintings such as 'The Fascists Flee From Novgorod' (1944–6, RM).

Although, inevitably, scenes of war, patriotism and overt anti-German propaganda dominated the Soviet artistic arena, there were some important developments in other areas. Portraiture received serious attention from Konchalovsky, Sar'yan and Serov and added a valuable contribution to the traditions of the 1930s. Similarly, monumental painting was not neglected thanks in particular to the completion of further stations on the

Moscow metro in 1943 and 1944 – these required marble and smalt decorations, the most notable being the *plafonds* or ceiling decorations by Deineka on Novokuznetskaya Station.

The post-war period was one of the most barren in the history of Soviet art, haunted as it was by the severe and conservative Zhdanov administration. Scenes of war became suddenly retrospective and isolated events now took on a broader, more symbolic meaning, with the result that an element of romanticism, even of sentimentalism, became apparent in many of the war pictures of the mid-1940s, e.g. 'Glory to the Fallen Heroes' (1945, TG) by F. S. Bogorodsky (1895–1960) and the moving 'Last Days' (1948, TG) by the Kukryniksy. This change of emphasis, however interesting in itself, served to lessen the impact of what in the 1930s had been a very direct and powerful Realism. In this sense the post-war and modern periods have been similar to the 1880s when the canons of Realism in the visual arts were already weakened to a marked extent and degraded, a development exemplified by such pictures as Plastov's

Kukryniksy (M. V. Kupriyanov, P. N. Krylov and N. A. Sokolov), cover to *Krokodil*, 1943, entitled: 'I lost my little ring . . . (and in my ring are 22 divisions)'.

'A Tractor Driver's Supper' (1951, TG). In the late 1940s and early 1950s a new departure was observed in the formal approach to depictions of the last war especially in the employment of panoramas and dioramas to transmit the grandeur and momentum of that historic period. Students of the Grekov studio, for example, created a gigantic circlorama 4 metres high, 22 metres long and one-fifth of natural size entitled 'Battle of the Volga' (1948–50, Volgograd). This innovation affected other branches of the visual arts – monumental art indeed became monumental as the first stations on the Leningrad metro and new ones on the Moscow network provided ample space for large-scale depictions of the war and Russian history. But even in this field a certain absence of content and a tendency towards exaggerated symbolism and decorativism were noticeable; and despite official criticism of this,[12] the trend continues today, as the mo-

Erik Bulatov, 'Self-portrait' (1968).

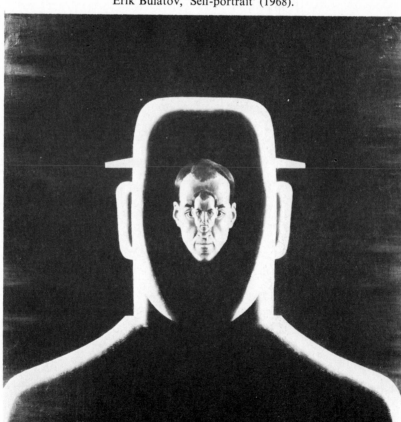

[12] See Party Decree of 4 November 1955, 'On the Elimination of Excesses in Design and Construction' (Ob ustranenii izlishestv v proyektirovanii i stroitel'stve).

saics on the Pioneer Palace and SEV building in Moscow demonstrate so clearly.

The last fifteen years or so have witnessed a gradual, although sporadic relaxation of official policy on the Soviet visual arts. The personality cult which inspired the interminable portraits of Stalin has ceased and artistic energies have been redirected into a new interest in Lenin and scenes from the Revolution and the Civil War. But perhaps the most striking developments, at least in painting, graphics, sculpture and design, have been in the world of 'unofficial' art, even though such works rely for their effect more on socio-political themes than on formal innovation, i.e. one tends to *read* them rather than *see* them. Mikhail Shemyakin (b. 1943) and his daughter Dorothée (b. 1964) (both now living in Paris), Ernst Neizvestny (b. 1926, now living in Zürich and New York), Lev Nusberg (b. 1936, now living in Paris), Oskar Rabin (b. 1928), Yevgeny Rukhin (1943–76), Boris Sveshnikov (b. 1927) and Vladimir Yakovlev (b. 1937) have received publicity, negative and positive, both in the Soviet Union and in the west, although the work of many of their colleagues still remains unrecognized. The so-called Manège affair in 1962, at which Khrushchev violently condemned abstract and semi-abstract works on view,[13] was the first of a series of open conflicts between the Establishment and the network of unorthodox directions

Francisco Infante, 'Beads'. From the series *The Architecture of Artificial Systems in Cosmic Space* (1972).

[13] For the text of Khrushchev's statement see 'Khrushchev on Modern Art', in *Encounter*, London, 1963, no. 115, pp. 102–3.

which threaten to widen still further the gap between official doctrine and artistic practice. Soviet artists, art historians and collectors are becoming more familiar with their dynamic heritage of the first quarter of the century and are coming into closer contact with the western *avant-garde*. The results of this aesthetic combination are, in some cases, truly remarkable, as, for example, in the kinetic works of Francisco Infante (b. 1943) and his kinetic group known as ARGO (Avtorskaya rabochaya gruppa [lit. Author Working Group]). Consequently, the position of Socialist Realism as the only available artistic discipline is now very precarious. All signs point to a crisis of style, one which can be overcome either by a renewal of cultural despotism or by a drastic liberalization of artistic procedure.

Architecture

The years immediately after the 1917 Revolution were decisive and transformative in the field of theoretical architecture but, at first at least, not fruitful in actual construction. In the first half of the 1920s many audacious and original projects were advanced, yet only a small number of them was realized either because of economic factors or because the plans were totally impracticable.

During this early period the main problem which faced the Soviet architect was that of housing, a matter to which the Party gave primary consideration – slum clearance, the construction of house communes and general urban replanning were the most urgent tasks of the day – while more specific enterprises such as work palaces and administrative centres (e.g. Tatlin's Tower) were deferred or annulled. A question of secondary but still major importance which beset the architect and engineer was Lenin's call for the electrification of the country: this led directly to the projection and realization of several hydroelectric stations such as at Shatura near Moscow in 1920 and, much later, on the Dnieper (1929–32), the latter designed by V. A. Vesnin (1882–1950) and others; other electrical installations such as V. G. Shukhov's radio tower in Moscow (1922) should also be mentioned. Essentially, many of the architectural achievements of the first five years were of questionable artistic value, and the barrack-like appearance of the many new tenement houses well reflected the architect's exclusive attention to basic needs divested of aesthetic considerations. The effect of the stringent economic conditions was described succinctly by two of the Vesnin brothers and Ginzburg: 'one had to reduce the cost of every cubic metre of construction, to economize on every barrel of cement, on every pound of nails'.[14] Moreover, when building programmes

[14] V. and A. Vesnin and M. Ginzburg, 'Problemy sovetskoy arkhitektury', in *Arkhitektura SSSR*, Moscow, 1934, no. 2, p. 69. Quoted from I. Grabar' *et al.* (ed.), *Istoriya russkogo iskusstva*, Moscow, 1957, vol. XI, p. 509.

Vladimir Tatlin, 'Monument to the Third International' (1919–20).

began to materialize after the early 1920s, many important designs were allotted to those architects who had already established themselves well before the Revolution, such as Fomin, V. A. Shchuko (1878–1939), Shchusev and Zholtovsky. Because of their conservative inclinations their projects tended to adopt principles of the Classical revivals rather than of any progressive directions, and it was thanks partly to the continued dominance of such architects that the grand, anachronistic 'palaces' which began with the 1930s continued to be built until the early 1950s. However, initially at least, some of these more conventional architects did not yield completely to eclecticism and decorativism and, at times, managed to maintain a rationality and purity of line identifiable in turn with the Constructivist movement: L. V. Rudnyov, for example, with the later help of Fomin designed the simple and spacious monument 'To the Victims of the Revolution' in Petrograd (1917–19) and Shchusev designed the constructivistic Lenin Mausoleum in Moscow (wooden version in 1924, stone in 1929–30).

By 1922 a new architecture had begun to take shape. The worst effects of the Civil War had passed and the economic situation was stronger. In addition, a young generation of architects had begun to assert themselves, sharing the same radical ideas as their colleagues Lissitzky, Tatlin, etc. There were now more architectural possibilities, more materials and,

Lenin Mausoleum, Moscow (A. V. Shchusev, 1929–30).

although the problem of living accommodation was still acute, other types of building were given serious attention: industry demanded new projects, government administration required new premises, new towns and satellite areas were planned and developed, e.g. Magnitogorsk, Stalino, Kuznetsk. Because of the extensive need for designs and, one should add, because of the sympathy of Narkompros, many leftists were enabled to submit projects and, quite often, to see them realized, e.g. the pavilions for the All-Russian Agricultural Exhibition in Moscow (1923) and for the Inter-

Moscow, *Izvestiya* building (G. B. Barkhin, 1927).

national Exhibition of Decorative Arts in Paris, both by K. S. Mel'nikov
(1890-1974), and the famous *Izvestiya* building in Moscow (1927) by
G. B. Barkhin. The dominant influence assimilated by the progressive
architects was Constructivism with its emphasis on function and rationality. Despite its advantages, Constructivism in architecture did, however,
tend to neglect artistic heritage and environmental factors, so that many
Soviet Constructivist buildings, while intrinsically good, relate badly to
their immediate contexts: Barkhin's *Izvestiya* building, for example,
clashes with the pre-Revolutionary buildings which still stand nearby.
Admittedly, this attitude did stem in part from the fact that many local
environments of the larger cities were scheduled for reconstruction; but,
again, this overall policy, when implemented, destroyed much of historical
and restorational value, a tradition which has been sadly observed until
only recently.

But whatever the faults of the leftist architects their contribution to the
universal development of modern architecture was unequivocal, and
their intense concern with modern materials – concrete, steel, glass – their
concentration on the convenience and expediency of space and their
orientation towards the machine and industry indicated the directions
which modern western architecture would take.

Throughout the 1920s the Soviet progressive architects were in constant
touch with their western counterparts, and their main literary organ, *SA*
(*Sovremennaya arkhitektura*), carried articles and photographic material
on the latest American and western European achievements. But as with
Constructivists in other fields such as the theatre and literature, the *avant-
garde* architects were already losing ground by the late 1920s: their
principal societies, ASNOVA (Association of New Architects, 1923–32)
and OSA (Union of Contemporary Architects, 1925–32), lost their independence, *SA* collapsed in 1930, while the government came increasingly
to condemn Constructivism as 'formalist' and devoid of socialist content.
Consequently, by the late 1920s Constructivism was beginning to lose
political favour, as shown by the official predilection for such eclectic
buildings as the Central Telegraph in Moscow (I. I. Rerberg, 1925–7),
the Lenin Library (Shchuko, V. G. Gel'freykh, 1928–40) and the many
fanciful projects for the Palace of Soviets (1930–3). In 1932 thanks to the
Decree, 'On the Reconstruction of Literary and Art Organizations', and
the proposed establishment of a single Union of Soviet Architects, Constructivism as a feasible art form was virtually discontinued.

The 1930s witnessed the extensive construction of large-scale projects
of the domestic, administrative and industrial type. The hall-mark of such
buildings was the Palladian or neo-Classical style, the clarity of Constructivism giving way to a more ornamental approach. A decisive impetus
to the realization of many such buildings was afforded by the proposal to

replan Moscow (and to a lesser extent Leningrad) which took effect between 1936 and 1945. The 1931 Decree of the Party which temporarily forbade extensive industrial construction in the two capitals also inspired the creation of a number of new industrial complexes away from the big towns. The demand for industrial designs attracted the more progressive architects such as the Vesnins and Ya. G. Chernikhov (1889–1951) while domestic needs were served by the more conservative.

However unsatisfactory or even pernicious the results of architectural developments in the 1930s, they did, in general, reflect the urgent desire of a new power to assert itself. Nowhere was this more evident than in the project for a Palace of Soviets drawn up by B. M. Iofan, Gel'freykh and Shchuko in 1932–3: this was to have been at least 400 metres high and surmounted by a statue of Lenin a further 100 metres high. But the project was modified and then ultimately cancelled because of many complicated problems concerning such varied aspects as the building's foundations and the fear that low cloud might obscure the statue of Lenin. Nevertheless, the morose grandeur and monumentality of this gigantic structure were maintained in such schemes as the Moscow hotel, 'Moskva' (Shchusev et al., completed in 1938), the nearby House of the Council of Ministers (A. Ya. Langman, 1933–6) and the Gor'ky Street complex (A. G. Mordvinov et al., 1941). These huge piles rose at the expense of widespread demolition not only of whole areas of wooden houses and shops but also of historic relics; for example, the drive for reconstruction in Moscow destroyed the famous Red Gates, the Sukharev Tower and part of the Simonov Monastery.

The first trains ran on the Moscow metro in 1935. Such stations as Komsomol'skaya, Ploshchad' Sverdlova (Fomin's last work) and Dzerzhinskaya (by the Constructivist, N. A. Ladovsky), however provocative in style, were a great improvement on the confined, ill-lit stations of the London and New York networks: the spaciousness and easy access to trains were architectural prerequisites which today, in more crowded times, are vastly appreciated. The same can be said of the substantial improvement and expansion of the ring road system in Moscow and of the several impressive bridges such as the Krymskiy Most (B. P. Konstantinov et al.) constructed during the mid- and late 1930s. The prevailing concern with space was also evident in the reconstructed Likhachev car plant in Moscow (A. S. Fisenko et al.) and the Kirov meat combine in Leningrad (N. A. Trotsky), although little attention was paid to their integration with the immediate landscape.

Although architectural development was severely curtailed by the Second World War, it was not confined exclusively to the planning of field hospitals, bunkers or other front-line apparatus. Because of the immediate threat to Leningrad, Stalingrad and Moscow, many important

169

industrial complexes were transferred to the east and in some cases completely new enterprises were realized, particularly in Central Asia. This in turn led to the formation of new settlements, rapidly planned ·and constructed, such as Gur'evo (1943), as well as to the industrialization of virgin lands; but, inevitably, the general quality of such new developments was poor because relevant materials were needed at the front and local replacements were often totally inadequate. Before the end of the war projects for the reconstruction of damaged towns had been undertaken already – the rebuilding of Stalingrad, for example, was planned as early as 1943 and of Novgorod in 1945. This is not to say that all architectural activity outside of military concerns was channelled into the removal of vulnerable plants or the projected reconstruction of urban centres, for a certain amount of building continued even in the more westerly cities: it was during the war years, in fact, that seven more stations were opened on the Moscow metro, including Avtozavodskaya and Novokuznetskaya.

The immediate post-war period was devoted primarily to reconstruction and restoration, a task facilitated in the case of historic buildings such as Peterhof by the fact that extensive measurements and detailed photographs had often been taken at the beginning of the war; and, although at times too obviously imitative, Soviet attempts at palatial restoration are to be applauded. The end of the 1940s and beginning of the 1950s marked a further stage in the construction of massive tenement blocks in the cities. The policy of monumentality was sustained and produced the series of 'wedding-cakes' – such as Moscow University (Rudnyov *et al.*,

Yakov Chernikhov, 'Complex Constructive Composition in an Axonometric Depiction'.

Komsomol'skaya Station on the Moscow metro (D. N. Chechulin, 1935).

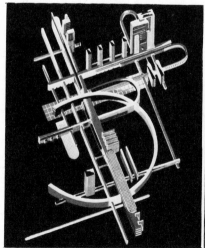

1953) and the Moscow hotel, the Ukraina (Mordvinov, 1956) – and the first of the *mikrorayony* (city districts) such as the Novyye Cheryomushki suburb of Moscow.

The late 1950s saw a distinct change in architectural policy due undoubtedly to the partial cultural liberalization which took place after the accession of Khrushchev. As western ideas were assimilated, the catholicity of the buildings of the Stalin period began to give way to a renewed purity

Moscow, Hotel Ukraina (A. G. Mordvinov *et al.*, 1956).

of line: 1961 witnessed the completion of the ·much debated Palace of Congresses in the Kremlin (Posokhin *et al.*) and the following year of the spacious cinema, the Rossiya (Sheverdyazev *et al.*), also in Moscow. The revival of the best traditions of the progressive architecture of the 1920s – the preoccupation with function, with rationality, with application of glass – has taken place over the last decade or so: the ponderous labyrinth of the Hotel Rossiya (D. N. Chechulin and others, 1968) which unfortunately impairs the general architectural cohesion of Red Square, the Novyy Arbat complex (which Posokhin and others derived from a Constructivist design of 1923 for a City of the Future, 1968–9) and the ill-positioned annexe to the Hotel Natsional' (opened 1970, Voskresensky and others), point both to rapid familiarization with the latest constructional techniques and to a modern conception of the role of architecture in an industrialized society. Provided that this conception is expanded to include serious environmental study, landscape planning and amelioration of construction materials, we may hope for a positive international contribution by new Soviet architecture.

The New Arbat complex, view of Kalinin Prospekt (M. V. Posokhin *et al.*, 1969).

GUIDE TO FURTHER READING

Note: the titles listed below form only a selective list. For a comprehensive and detailed bibliography of works on Russian art of the late nineteenth and twentieth centuries (both in Russian and in non-Russian languages), the student is advised to consult the bibliographical sections in *Russian Art of the Avant-Garde: Theory and Criticism 1902–1934*, edited by John E. Bowlt, New York, 1976, pp. 309–48.

ART

General works, in Russian

Istoriya russkogo iskusstva, ed. I. E. Grabar' *et al.*, Akademiya Nauk SSSR, Moscow, vol. IX, bks. 1 and 2 (1965); vol. X, bk. 1 (1968), bk. 2 (1969); vol. XI (1957); vol. XI (1961); vol. XIII (1964).

These volumes vary in quality a great deal. Those concerned with the periods 1907–17 (vol. X, bk. 2) and 1917–21 (vol. XI) are not detailed and at times are factually inaccurate. Vol. IX (on the late nineteenth century) is comprehensive. In all cases reproductions are mediocre.

Mastera iskusstva ob iskusstve. Iskusstvo kontsa XIX – nachala XX veka, Moscow, 1969, vol. 7.

This contains extracts from letters, diaries and articles by important painters of the period including Borisov-Musatov, Kuznetsov, Larionov, Shevchenko and Vrubel'.

Russkaya khudozhestvennaya kul'tura kontsa XIX – nachala XX veka, ed. A. D. Alekseyev *et al.*, Moscow, bk. 1, 1968, bk. 2, 1969, bk. 3, 1978.

These three volumes comprise the first detailed Soviet monograph on Modernism in the visual arts and music. The work is scholarly, especially on the 'World of Art' movement, and betrays a distinct shift of critical focus *vis-à-vis* previous texts on the subject.

A. Benois, *Istoriya russkoy zhivopisi v XIX veke*, St Petersburg, 1901–2 (2 vols.).

A straightforward and clear presentation of the main Russian art movements in the nineteenth century. The author's awareness of parallel western trends gives the book added dimension. Translated as *History of Russian Painting*, New York, 1916.

L. D'yakonitsyn, *Ideynyye protivorechiya v estetike russkoy zhivopisi kontsa 19 – nachala 20 vv.*, Perm', 1966.

The book's main value is its frequent recourse to archival quotations, but much information is inaccurate (e.g. dates, contributors to exhibitions).

A. Efros, *Dva veka russkogo iskusstva*, Moscow, 1969.

An important, but neglected, book on Russian art of the eighteenth and nineteenth centuries. Based on manuscripts of this incisive critic and published posthumously.

A. Fyodorov-Davydov, *Russkoye iskusstvo promyshlennogo kapitalizma*, Moscow, 1929.

Especially useful for statistics on the growth of the Russian art market during the second half of the nineteenth century.

V. Lobanov, *Khudozhestvennyye gruppirovki za posledniye 25 let*, Moscow, 1930.

Detailed presentation of the main groups and exhibitions of the Modernist period. Factually accurate.

173

S. Makovsky, *Stranitsy khudozhestvennoy kritiki*, bk. 2, St Petersburg, 1909; bk. 3, St Petersburg, 1911.

These volumes are based on Makovsky's articles and exhibition reviews which appeared in various journals in the 1900s. Valuable as a 'first-hand account'.

N. Mashkovtsev (ed.), *Ocherki po istorii russkogo portreta vtoroy poloviny XIX veka*, Moscow, 1963.

A serious study of the portraits of the principal Wanderers.

N. Mashkovtsev and N. Sokolova (ed.), *Ocherki po istorii russkogo portreta kontsa XIX – nachala XX veka*, Moscow, 1964.

Contains chapters on Serov, Serebryakova, Somov, Vrubel' and others.

N. Moleva and I. Belyutin, *Russkaya khudozhestvennaya shkola vtoroy poloviny XIX– nachala XX veka*, Moscow, 1967.

An informative, but tedious, monograph on the primary and secondary Realists. Nothing of value on movements after 1900.

D. V. Sarab'yanov, *Russkaya zhivopis' kontsa 1900-kh – nachala 1910-kh godov*, Moscow, 1971.

A collection of essays on progressive painters including P. Kuznetsov, Larionov and Fal'k. A positive and analytical study.

S. Shcherbatov, *Khudozhnik v ushedshey Rossii*, New York, 1955.

Reminiscences by an associate of the 'World of Art' painters, but no hard facts are given. Nothing at all on the *avant-garde*.

General works, in other languages

T. Andersen, *Moderne russisk kunst, 1910–1930*, Copenhagen, 1967.

Despite its poor illustrations this work is the most scholarly and accurate of all books on the *avant-garde* so far published.

A. Benois, *The Russian School of Painting*, New York, 1916.

A version of the *Istoriya russkoy zhivopisi v XIX veke*.

J. Bowlt, *Russian Art of the Avant-Garde: Theory and Criticism 1902–1934*, New York, 1976.

A collection of artists' and critics' manifestoes and statements covering the *avant-garde* period; in English, with notes and extensive bibliography.

C. Gray, *The Great Experiment. Russian Art 1863–1922*, London, 1962. New edn, 1971, as *The Russian Experiment in Art, 1863–1922*. A general survey of Modernist Russian art with particular stress on movements after 1912. Illustrations are of excellent quality.

A. del Guercio, *Le avanguardie russe e sovietiche*, Milan, 1970.

The text is mediocre, but the illustrations, mostly in good colour, are comprehensive.

G. Loukomski, *History of Modern Russian Painting, 1840–1940*, London, 1945.

As a handbook useful for developments up to *c.* 1900, but unreliable after that.

V. Marcadé, *Le Renouveau de l'art pictural russe*, Lausanne, 1971.

A detailed survey of the early Modernist period. More important than the text or (poor) reproductions are the addenda of catalogue lists and bibliography.

L. Réau, *L'Art russe de Pierre le Grand à nos jours*, Paris, 1922.

Emphasis is on the eighteenth and nineteenth centuries and little of value is provided on *nos jours*. This book is reprinted together with his *L'art russe des origines à Pierre le Grand* (Paris, 1921) as *L'Art russe* (3 vols.), Paris, 1968.

H. Rubissow, *The Art of Russia*, New York, 1946.

The text is worthless, but the monochrome illustrations provide rare examples of easel painting after 1925 and during the early 1930s.

Russian Avant-garde, 1908–1921. Catalogue of exhibition at the Leonard Hutton
Galleries, New York, October 1971 – February 1972. New York, 1971.

W. Schmidt, *Russische Graphik des XIX. und XX. Jahrhunderts*, Leipzig, 1967.
A large descriptive catalogue of a certain Berlin collection of graphics. The author
concentrates on the first thirty years of the twentieth century and much information is
given on the lesser members of the *avant-garde*. Illustrations, colour and monochrome, are good.

O. Wulff, *Die neurussische Kunst im Rahmen der Kulturentwicklung Russlands von Peter
dem Grossen bis zur Revolution*, Augsburg, 1932.
A scholarly work which attempts a comparative examination of Russian painting, but
the text is marred by wrong dates, wrong attributions and poor reproductions.

Specific works

The student is advised to consult relevant chapters in the above-mentioned works as well
as titles listed below.

The Wanderers and Realism, in Russian

A. Fyodorov-Davydov, *Realizm v russkoy zhivopisi XIX veka*, Moscow, 1933.

Ya. Minchenkov, *Vospominaniya o peredvizhnikakh*, Leningrad, 1964.

A. Novitsky, *Peredvizhniki i vliyaniye ikh na russkoye iskusstvo*, Moscow, 1897.

D. Sarab'yanov, *Narodno-osvoboditel'nyye idei russkoy zhivopisi vtoroy poloviny XIX
veka,* Moscow, 1955.
A scholarly book with valuable pages on Surikov and Repin.

V. Ziloti, *V dome Tret'yakova*, New York, 1954.
Provides information on many of the Wanderers and their relations with Tret'yakov.

The Wanderers and Realism, in other languages

V. Fiala, *Die russische realistische Malerei des 19. Jahrhunderts*, Prague, 1953.

Neo-nationalism, in Russian

I. Belogortsev, *Talashkino*, Smolensk, 1950.

D. Kogan, *Mamontovskiy kruzhok*, Moscow, 1970.
A general history of Mamontov and Abramtsevo. Illustrations are poor.

M. Kopshitser, *Mamontov*, Moscow, 1969.
Detailed appraisal of Savva Mamontov and Abramtsevo.

S. Makovsky and N. Rerikh, *Talashkino. Izdeliya masterskikh kn. M. Kl. Tenishevoy*,
St Petersburg, 1905.
A detailed survey of the Talashkino colony. Text is authoritative and illustrations,
colour and monochrome, are good.

N. Pakhomov, *Abramtsevo*, Moscow, 1969.

N. Polenova, *Abramtsevo. Vospominaniya*, Moscow, 1922.
Provides intimate details of Abramtsevo figures, especially of the Polenovs and V.
Vasnetsov.

B. Rybchenkov and A. Chaplin, *Talashkino*, Moscow, 1973.
A useful book on the history of Talashkino both in Russian and in Soviet times.

M. Tenisheva, *Vpechatleniya moey zhizni*, Paris, 1933.
Interesting, but 'coloured', recollections of the princess' activities in the St Petersburg
art world and at Talashkino.

Neo-nationalism, in other languages

S. Makovsky et N. Roerikh, *Talachkino. L'Art décoratif des ateliers de la Princesse
Tenicheva*, St Petersburg, 1906.

The 'World of Art', in Russian

Mir iskusstva, St Petersburg, 1898–1904 (last numbers for 1904 appeared, in fact, only in 1905).

The literary organ of the 'World of Art' group, this journal presented articles on many aspects of Modernist art both of Russia and of western Europe.

Apollon, St Petersburg, 1909–17 (last numbers for 1917 appeared, in fact, only in 1918).

The platform for several artistic and literary tendencies, this journal also did much to advance the cause of the second generation of 'World of Art' painters.

A. Benois, *Vozniknoveniye Mira iskusstva*, Leningrad, 1928.

The first authoritative description of the genesis and development of the 'World of Art'.

M. Dobuzhinsky, 'Krug "Mir iskusstva"', *Novyy zhurnal*, New York, 1942, no. 3, pp. 312–36.

A. Gusarova, *Mir iskusstva*, Leningrad, 1972.

V. Petrov, *Mir iskusstva. Le Monde artiste*, Moscow, 1975.

An album of colour illustrations with preface in Russian and French.

A. Sidorov, *Russkaya grafika nachala XX veka*, Moscow, 1969.

A sympathetic presentation of the graphic work of the artists of the 'World of Art' and 'Golden Fleece' circles. Excellent illustrations.

N. Sokolova, *Mir iskusstva*, Moscow–Leningrad, 1934.

Despite the date of publication, still a very useful survey of the 'World of Art'.

G. Sternin, *Khudozhestvennaya zhizn' Rossii na rubezhe XIX–XX vekov*, Moscow, 1970.

Takes a much more positive approach to the question than previous Soviet publications. Many archival quotations.

A. Strelkov, *Mir iskusstva*, Moscow–Petrograd, 1923.

The 'World of Art', in other languages

A. Benois, *Reminiscences of the Russian Ballet*, London, 1941.

J. Bowlt, 'The World of Art', *Russian Literature Triquarterly*, Ann Arbor, 1972, Fall no., pp. 183–218.

A survey of the literary and painting achievements of this group.

A. Haskell, *Diaghileff. His Artistic and Private Life*, London, 1955.

Still the most reliable portrait of Diaghilev both in the early and later years. Factual accuracy is ensured by the recourse to Walter Nouvel's unpublished manuscript on Diaghilev.

The 'Blue Rose' and Symbolism, in Russian

Iskusstvo, Moscow, 1905 (7 issues only).

This journal, edited by N. Tarovaty, advanced the cause of the future 'Blue Rose' artists by publishing articles on Symbolism and art and by reproducing their paintings.

Vesy, Moscow, 1904–9.

Although primarily a literary journal, *Vesy* did much to encourage Russian Symbolist painting. Its graphic decoration by 'Blue Rose' and other painters was especially important in this respect.

Zolotoye runo, Moscow, 1906–9 (last numbers for 1909 appeared, in fact, only in 1910).

The literary organ of the 'Blue Rose' artists.

M. Alpatov, *P. V. Kuznetsov*, Moscow, 1968.

An album of reproductions which includes some early canvases. The text is insignificant.

M. Alpatov and E. Gunst, *N. N. Sapunov*, Moscow, 1965.

V. Lobanov, *Kanuny*, Moscow, 1968 (especially pp. 82–205).

Entertaining memoirs of a one-time newspaper art critic on groups and exhibitions of pre-Revolutionary Moscow. Factually not always reliable.

V. Midler (author of introduction), *Mastera 'Goluboy rozy', Katalog vystavki*, Moscow, 1925.

K. Petrov-Vodkin, *Prostranstvo Evklida*, Moscow, 1932. Re-edited in *Khlynovsk. Prostranstvo Evklida. Samarkandiya* (ed. by Yu. Rusakov), Leningrad, 1970.
Memoirs which demonstrate the painter's undoubted gift for creative writing. The text is illustrated by the author.

M. Sar'yan, *Iz moyey zhizni*, Moscow, 1970.
The first volume of Sar'yan's memoirs. Treats of his childhood and years at the Moscow Institute of Painting. Provides information on fellow members of the 'Blue Rose'.

Neo-primitivism and Cubo-futurism, in Russian

Soyuz molodyozhi, St Petersburg, 1912–13 (three issues in all).
Contains many interesting articles and reproductions. Of particular note are contributions by V. Markov and O. Rozanova.

D. Burlyuk, V. Mayakovsky *et al.*, *Poshchochina obshchestvennomu vkusu*, Moscow, 1912.
Apart from the famous manifesto, this miscellany contains two essays by D. Burlyuk on 'Texture' and 'Cubism'.

N. Goncharova, Introduction to catalogue of *Personal'naya vystavka*, Moscow, 1913.
One of Goncharova's rare published statements on art.

V. Kamensky, *Put' entuziasta*, Moscow, 1931, and *Zhizn' s Mayakovskim*, Moscow, 1940.
Both the Kamensky books, although dealing with literature rather than with the visual arts, provide information on the art exploits of the Futurists, especially of Larionov.

N. Khardzhiyev, 'Mayakovsky i zhivopis'', in *Mayakovsky. Materialy i issledovaniya*, Moscow, 1940, pp. 337–400.
Useful details on Mayakovsky's abortive stay at the Moscow Institute of Painting and his relations with the Burlyuks, Larionov, etc.

M. Larionov, 'Luchistskaya zhivopis'', *Oslinyy khvost i mishen'*, Moscow, 1913, pp. 83–124.
The Rayonist manifesto; also published as *Luchizm*, Moscow, 1913.

B. Livshits, *Polutoraglazyy strelets*, Leningrad, 1933. French translation by E. Sébald, V. and J. C. Marcadé, *L'Archer à un œil et demi*, Lausanne, 1971. English translation by John E. Bowlt, *The One and a Half-eyed Archer*, Newtonville, 1977.
A Futurist's memoirs of Futurism especially as it affected painting. Intimate details of the Burlyuks, Ekster and Puni.

V. Parkin (ed.), *Oslinyy khvost i mishen'*, Moscow, 1913.
This miscellany contains both Larionov's Rayonist manifesto and his declaration 'Luchisty i budushchniki'.

A. Shevchenko, *Neo-primitivizm*, Moscow, 1913.
Despite its late appearance, this can be taken as the apology of the Neo-primitivists, although it examines the genesis of Neo-primitivism rather than its aims and aspirations.

A. Shevchenko, *Printsipy kubizma i drugikh sovremennykh techeniy v zhivopisi vsekh vremyon i narodov*, Moscow, 1913.

G. Tasteven, *Futurizm*, Moscow, 1914.

Neo-primitivism and Cubo-futurism, in other languages

D. Burlyuk (ed.), *Color and Rhyme*, New York, 1930–66.
This journal, of fluctuating quality, published many articles and reproductions concerned with the origins and development of Russian Futurism. Some of the more

unusual contributions, such as Burlyuk's essay on Filonov (1954, no. 28), are entertaining, if unreliable.

M. Calvesi, 'Il futurismo russo' in *L'arte moderna*, Milan, 1967, vol. v, no. 44.

R. Carrieri, *Futurism*, Milan, 1963 (especially pp. 129–45).
Interesting as an examination of Russian Futurism *vis-à-vis* Italian, although, under-
standably, Russian artists are not given their full merit.

M. Chamot, *Gontcharova*, Paris, 1972.
Beautifully illustrated monograph on Gontcharova. General text in French.

W. George, *Larionov*, Paris, 1966; German edition, Frankfurt/Main, 1968.
Useful for reproductions, but factually unreliable.

V. Markov, *Russian Futurism*, Berkeley, 1968 and London, 1969.
Deals primarily with literary Futurism, although some space is devoted to the visual
arts. Invaluable for names and dates of both writers and artists.

Abstractionism, in Russian

E. Gollerbakh, 'Puti noveyshego iskusstva na Zapade i u nas' in *Istoriya iskusstv vsekh
vremyon i narodov*, bk. 5, Leningrad, 1929.
One of the last sympathetic descriptions of Modernism before the negative attitude of
the 1930s and 1940s. Authoritative and contains quotations from artists' statements.

I. Ioffe, *Krizis sovremennogo iskusstva*, Leningrad, 1925.

S. Makovsky, *Posledniye itogi zhivopisi*, Berlin, 1922.

I. Puni (J. Pougny), *Sovremennaya zhivopis'*, Berlin, 1923.
An analytical approach to Suprematism and other movements by a pioneer of Abstractionism.

N. Punin, *Noveyshiye techeniya v russkom iskusstve*, Leningrad, 1927/8.
One of Punin's finest critical works.

(For Malevich and Tatlin see next section.)

Abstractionism, in other languages

H. Berninger and J. P. Cartier, *Pougny. Catalogue de l'œuvre. Russie–Berlin 1910–1923*,
Tübingen, 1972.
Invaluable monograph on Pougny and his colleagues; complemented by excellent
reproductions.

K. Malevich, *Essays* (English translation of Malevich's major essays, ed. T. Andersen),
Copenhagen, 1968.

K. Malevich, Catalogue of collection at the Stedelijk Museum, Amsterdam, Amsterdam,
1970.
Compiled by T. Andersen, this catalogue is very informative, accurate and provides
much new material on Malevich's painting and theories. Reproductions, colour and
monochrome, are good.

V. Tatlin, Catalogue of exhibition at the Moderna Museet, Stockholm, 1968.
Compiled by T. Andersen, this catalogue presents both bio-bibliographical details and
critical commentary.

K. Umansky, *Neue Kunst in Russland, 1914–1919*, Munich, 1920.

G. Veronesi, 'Suprematisti e construttivisti in Russia' in *L'arte moderna*, Milan, 1967,
vol. vi, no. 48.

Art and Revolution, in Russian

Iskusstvo kommuny, Petrograd, 1918–19.
One of several short-lived, but dynamic, journals which were created immediately after
1917. Contained contributions by Al'tman, Brik, Punin and others.

Izobrazitel'noye iskusstvo, Petrograd, 1919.

Russkoye iskusstvo, Petrograd, 1923.

ART

B. Arvatov, *Iskusstvo i klassy*, Moscow–Petrograd, 1923.
A sociological and stimulating approach to art of before and after the Revolution. Of especial interest are the author's remarks on Constructivism.
A. Galushkina (ed.) *et al., Agitatsionno-massovoye iskusstvo pervykh let Oktyabrya*, Moscow, 1971.
A detailed and scholarly study of the revolutionary posters, panneaux and *agit-transport*. Richly illustrated.
A. Lunacharsky, *Iskusstvo i revolyutsiya*, Moscow, 1924.
I. Matsa (ed.) *et al., Sovetskoye iskusstvo za 15 let*, Moscow, 1933.
Invaluable as a reference book for declarations and exhibitions of non-representational and representational groups in the 1920s.

Constructivism

Lef, Moscow, 1923–5, *Novyy lef*, Moscow, 1927–8.
Advanced the causes of Constructivism and post-revolutionary Futurism. Contains contributions by Brik, Kushner, Mayakovsky *et al*. Reproductions of Rodchenko's photographs are of particular significance.
Ya. Chernikhov, *Konstruktsiya arkhitekturnykh i mashinnykh form,* Leningrad, 1930 (re-ed., 1931).
Essentially a textbook for students of architecture and engineering, but important as an explanation and advocation of Constructivisim. Richly illustrated.
A. Gan, *Konstruktivizm*, Tver', 1922.
Can be regarded as the Constructivists' manifesto.
M. Ginzburg, *Stil' i epokha*, Moscow, 1924.
Basically an architectural explanation of Constructivism, but the sociological commentaries are valuable.
(For further references to Constructivism see the section on Architecture, 1917–73, below.)

Art and Revolution, in other languages

Cimaise, Paris, 1968, no. 85/86.
The whole issue is devoted to the *avant-garde*, especially of the 1920s. Well illustrated.
Výtvarné umění, Prague, 1967, no. 8/9.
The whole issue is devoted to the *avant-garde*. Especially valuable for material on Tatlin and Malevich.
S. Bojko, *New Graphic Design in Revolutionary Russia*, New York, 1972.
J. Freeman *et al., Voices of October*, New York, 1930.
Contains a chapter on general developments in the 1920s.
R. Fülöp-Miller, *The Mind and Face of Bolshevism*, London, 1927.
Contains a chapter on the organization and practice of art under the Communists, and useful descriptions of Tatlin's tower and comments on Efros, Lunacharsky *et al.*
C. Gray-Prokofieva (author of introduction), Catalogue of exhibition 'Art in Revolution' at the Hayward Gallery, London, 1971.
Provides little new information on painting and architecture in the 1920s, although the section on the cinema is valuable.
R. Lorenz (ed.), *Proletarische Kulturrevolution in Sowjetrussland* (1917–21), Munich, 1969.
Important documents (decrees, manifestos, etc.) pertaining to the reorganization of art after 1917. Some commentary, but not enough.
L. Lozowick, *Modern Russian Art*, New York, 1925.

Constructivism

(For references see the section on Architecture, 1917–73, below.)

Modern Russian Art (1932–73), in Russian

Dekorativnoye iskusstvo, Moscow, 1957–.
Iskusstvo, Moscow, 1933–.
Khudozhnik, Moscow, 1958–.
Tvorchestvo, Moscow, 1956–.
   All the above journals have articles on art and artists both of the pre- and post-revolutionary periods. *Dekorativnoye iskusstvo* is the most progressive.
A. Fyodorov-Davydov, *Sovetskiy peyzazh*, Moscow, 1958.
R. Kaufman, *Sovetskaya tematicheskaya kartina, 1917–1941*, Moscow, 1951.
P. Sysoyev and V. Shkvarikov, *Mastera sovetskogo izobrazitel'nogo iskusstva. Proizve-deniya i avtobiograficheskiye ocherki. Zhivopis'*, Moscow, 1951.
   Useful biographical details of modern Russian painters.

Modern Russian Art (1932–73), in other languages

C. Holme, *Art in the USSR* (Studio Special), London, 1935.
H. Lehmann-Haupt, *Art under a Dictatorship*, New York, 1954.
   Contains a section on art in the Soviet Union, but lacks inside information.
K. London, *The Seven Soviet Arts*, London, 1937, New York, 1938.
   Useful information on the structure of the proposed Union of Soviet Artists and some illustrations of unorthodox pictures.
P. Sjeklocha and I. Mead, *Unofficial Art in the Soviet Union*, Berkeley, 1967.
   Many statements are factually inaccurate, but reproductions of modern leftist paintings are valuable.
I. Weinke, *Sowjetische Malerei der Gegenwart*, Leipzig, 1967.

ARCHITECTURE

General works, in Russian

Istoriya russkogo iskusstva. Akademiya Nauk SSSR, Moscow, vol. ix, bk. 2 (1965); vol. x, bk. 2 (1969); vol. xi (1957); vol. xii (1961).
   See comments on these volumes in section on Art above.
Yu. Savitsky, *Russkoye klassicheskoye nalediye i sovremennaya arkhitektura*, Moscow, 1953.

General works, in other languages

A. Voyce, *Russian Architecture. Trends in Nationalism and Modernism*, New York, 1948.
   The text is mediocre, but contains valuable illustrations, especially of post-revolutionary buildings.

Specific works

The student is advised to consult relevant chapters in *Istoriya russkogo iskusstva* as well as titles listed below.

180

1860–1917, in Russian

Zodchiy, St Petersburg, 1872–1918.

The leading and most progressive architectural review of the time.

Russkaya khudozhestvennaya kul'tura kontsa XIX – nachala XX veka, Moscow, bk. 2, 1969.

Ye. Borisova and T. Kazhdan, *Russkaya arkhitektura kontsa XIX – nachala XX veka*, Moscow, 1970.

A serious study of art nouveau in architecture and interior decoration especially as it was applied to *osobnyaki* of Moscow and St Petersburg. Illustrations are poor.

1917–73, in Russian

Arkhitektura SSSR, Moscow, 1933–.

Sovremennaya arkhitektura, Moscow, 1926–1930.

Did much to advance the cause of Constructivism in architecture and allied arts. Contributions by the Vesnins, Gan, Ginzburg *et al.*

Sovetskaya arkhitektura. Yezhegodnik, Moscow, 1949–.

Arkhitektura SSSR. 1917–1947. Sbornik Soyuza sovetskikh arkhitektorov. No. 17/18, Moscow, 1947.

M. Barkhin (ed.), *Mastera sovetskoy arkhitektury ob arkhitekture*, 2 vols., Moscow, 1975.

An anthology of theoretical texts by leading Soviet architects.

V. Khazanova (compiler), *Iz istorii sovetskoy arkhitektury, 1917–1925*, Moscow, 1963.

Important documents, designs and photographs, mostly hitherto unpublished.

V. Khazanova, *Sovetskaya arkhitektura pervykh let Oktyabrya*, Moscow, 1970.

A historical survey of designs and projects until *c.* 1925. The attitude is positive and serious. Some unpublished material.

V. Kirillov (compiler), *Iz istorii sovetskoy arkhitektury, 1926–1932*, Moscow, 1970.

Has important material, both textual and visual. The attitude again is positive.

1917–73, in other languages

V. de Feo, *URSS. Architettura 1917–1936*, Rome, 1963.

A pioneer book in this area, but some mistakes and poor illustrations.

A. Kopp, *Town and Revolution. Soviet Architecture and City Planning, 1917–1935*, New York, 1970.

Much data including ground plans and general designs. Approach is sociological.

El Lissitzky, *Russland. Architektur für eine Weltrevolution*, Berlin, 1930 (re-ed., 1965).

Mainly illustrations of projects by Lissitzky and his colleagues. Second edition contains commentary and additional text.

V. Quilici, *Architettura sovietica contemporanea*, Bologna, 1965.

V. Quilici, *L'architettura del costruttivismo*, Bari, 1969.

Contains chapters on individual architects, including Mel'nikov and Ginzburg, as well as translations of statements.

A. Rosa *et al., Socialismo, città, architettura URSS, 1917–1937*, Rome, 1971.

O. Shvidkovsky, *Building in the USSR, 1917–1932*, London, 1971.

VH 101, Paris, 1972, no. 7–8.

Whole issue devoted to Soviet architecture, 1917–34, with many architectural statements of the time in translation.

INDEX

Numbers in italics refer to the illustrations

INDEX